Luminos is the Open Access monograph publishing program
from UC Press. Luminos provides a framework for preserving and
reinvigorating monograph publishing for the future and increases
the reach and visibility of important scholarly work. Titles published
in the UC Press Luminos model are published with the same high
standards for selection, peer review, production, and marketing as
those in our traditional program. www.luminosoa.org

Aspects of Kinship in Ancient Iran

IRAN IN THE ANCIENT WORLD

Iran and the Ancient World supports original studies in the history, literary traditions, material culture, and religions of ancient Iran, while seeking to relate these to the broader historiographic mainstream account of the ancient worlds. The series aims to foreground the interconnection of the Iranian world to other contiguous cultural expanses, fostering comparative and interdisciplinary perspectives on questions of broad import to the humanities and social sciences. The publisher and the University of California Press Foundation gratefully acknowledge the generous support for this series by the UCLA Pourdavoud Center for the Study of the Iranian World.

Series Editor: M. Rahim Shayegan, University of California, Los Angeles

Aspects of Kinship
in Ancient Iran

D. T. Potts

UNIVERSITY OF CALIFORNIA PRESS

University of California Press
Oakland, California

Suggested citation: Potts, D. T. *Aspects of Kinship in Ancient Iran*. Oakland:
University of California Press, 2023. DOI: https://doi.org/10.1525/luminos.164

Library of Congress Cataloging-in-Publication Data

Names: Potts, Daniel T., author.
Title: Aspects of kinship in ancient Iran / D. T. Potts.
Other titles: Iran in the ancient world ; 1.
Description: Oakland, [California] : University of California Press, [2023] |
    Series: Iran in the ancient world ; 1 | Includes bibliographical references
    and index.
Identifiers: LCCN 2023005937 (print) | LCCN 2023005938 (ebook) |
    ISBN 9780520394995 (paperback) | ISBN 9780520395015 (ebook)
    Subjects: LCSH: Kinship—Iran. | Iran—History—To 640.
Classification: LCC GN487 .P68 2023 (print) | LCC GN487 (ebook) |
    DDC 306.830935/7—dc23/eng/20230413

LC record available at https://lccn.loc.gov/2023005937
LC ebook record available at https://lccn.loc.gov/2023005938

Manufactured in the United States of America

32 31 30 29 28 27 26 25 24 23
10 9 8 7 6 5 4 3 2 1

CONTENTS

ILLUSTRATIONS

SERIES PREFACE

D. T. Potts' *Aspects of Kingship in Ancient Iran* is the inaugural volume of the newly established series Iran and the Ancient World, which supports original research foregrounding the interconnection of ancient Iran with other cultural expanses in antiquity.

The present volume represents the revised version of five lectures held at the University of California, Los Angeles in March 2020 as part of the Biennial Ehsan Yarshater Lecture Series. The publication of this volume was also made possible by support from the Institute for the Study of the Ancient World at New York University.

The Series Editor would like to acknowledge and thank the above institutions for their generous contributions.

M. Rahim Shayegan

The five chapters in this study represent lightly revised versions of the Biennial Ehsan Yarshater Lectures delivered at UCLA between 2 and 11 March 2020 under the auspices of the Pourdavoud Center for the Study of the Iranian World. I am indebted, first and foremost, to Professor Rahim Shayegan, the center's director, for the invitation to deliver these lectures and to the many friends and colleagues at UCLA who made the experience so memorable. Particular thanks go to Dr. Marissa Stevens of the Pourdavoud Center who organized so many things for my wife, Hildy, and me and made our stay so pleasant. For their generous assistance with images and information used in this work, I would also like to warmly acknowledge Javier Álvarez-Mon, Alireza Askari Chaverdi, John Ferreira, Wouter Henkelman, Brian Kritt, Dane Kuhrt, Fabrizio Sinisi, and Nikolaus Schindel. The comments of three anonymous readers on the original manuscript are also gratefully acknowledged.

Since their inception the Yarshater Lectures have been delivered on a wide range of topics, both ancient and modern, encompassing many different subfields of Iranian studies. I freely acknowledge that choosing a suitable topic was a considerable challenge, and it took some time before I settled on the broad theme of kinship. Although I had previously done some work on the avunculate (Potts 2018a), I had not worked extensively on kinship. Nevertheless, although it may not seem like an obvious choice of subject, kinship embodies the kind of historico-anthropological research that I enjoy, a branch of research that was absent from my education in what is termed "anthropological archaeology" at American universities. My own academic trajectory within Iranian studies has been characterized by many swings and roundabouts since I first began in the early 1970s as a student working on the

Bronze Age archaeology of southeastern Iran. From that time onward, my interests have steadily expanded and grown increasingly historical, to the point where they now encompass all periods of the pre-Islamic past, as well as the postconquest periods, right through the Qajar era (see Potts 2014, 2022a, and 2022b). I am far from expert in all of the periods in which I take an interest, but a fascination with Iran, as opposed to the discipline of archaeology per se, led me, many years ago, to begin pursuing a very different path from the one that my teachers and fellow students in anthropology probably anticipated. Instead of cleaving closely to the processual creed of American anthropological archaeology as taught to me between 1971 and 1980, I began moving into the domain of history, often assisted by epigraphic and literary sources, even before completing my dissertation. This inclination only intensified as a result of contact with Assyriologists in Copenhagen and Berlin between 1980 and 1991, when I became increasingly aware of the extraordinarily rich body of literary and epigraphic sources that offered a very different way of seeing the past than that in which I had been schooled. Since the mid-1990s, my work on the Elamites, Achaemenids, Seleucids, Arsacids, and Sasanians, as well as on nomadism and Safavid and Qajar history, has only pulled me further and further away from my American anthropological roots. Trips to Iran in 1995, 1996, and 2001 introduced me to both the architecture and the history of Safavid and Qajar Iran, and more recent work on eighteenth- and early nineteenth-century Iranian history has broadened my perspectives even further.

In thinking about what I might present, I had several considerations in mind. In the first place, I had no interest in offering something that might be broadly characterized as "traditionally archaeological"—that is, relating to excavations, typology, style, iconography, and so forth. Rather, I wanted to address issues that concerned the people of ancient Iran, drawing on a wide variety of sources, principally written, as opposed to their material culture. Moreover, I wanted to do something that was comparative, in the sense that it would illustrate how patterns observable in data from Iran belonged to a wider body of comparable material from outside Iran. In addition, like much of my work, I wished to offer a diachronic perspective, presenting cases drawn from many millennia of Iranian history. Specifically, I wanted to illustrate how a cross-cultural approach to Iranian data could help illuminate what have too often been viewed as peculiarly, even idiosyncratically, Iranian cultural practices. Finally, I wanted to attempt something in which the late Professor Yarshater would have taken an interest. Although I am neither a student of Persian literature nor Iranian linguistics, to name just two of his many fields, I was privileged to spend some precious hours with Professor Yarshater in his apartment on Riverside Drive and at the *Encyclopaedia Iranica* offices at Columbia over the past two decades, occasionally having lunch with him and talking about all manner of things. I remember well how honored I felt the first time I received an invitation from him to contribute to the *Encyclopaedia Iranica* and how much I looked forward to finally meeting him several years later. To sit with him in his office, aware of his immense erudition, was positively thrilling and only confirmed in my own mind that Iran and Iranology, rather than archaeology per se, were what mattered most to me. Little did I know at the time that the expansion of my interests from the archaeology of Bronze Age Iran to Safavid and Qajar history would only strengthen my resolve to devote as much of my scholarly energy to Iran as possible in the years to come.

But in addition to reflecting on Professor Yarshater, the invitation to deliver a series of lectures bearing his name prompted another kind of reflection. The intellectual history of Iranian studies has always been a subject of enormous interest to me, and I can think of dozens of intellectual companions in ancient Iranian studies who are never very far from my thoughts, scholars like Friedrich Carl Andreas, Wilhelm Eilers, Alfred von Gutschmid, Walter Bruno Henning, Ernst Herzfeld, Albert Houtum-Schindler, A. V. Williams Jackson, Ferdinand Justi, Josef Markwart, Vladimir Minorsky, Theodor Nöldeke, William Ouseley, Henry Rawlinson, Vincent Scheil, Marc Aurel Stein, Wilhelm Tomaschek, Rüdiger Schmitt, and Ran Zadok. They, too, crowded my mind when I began to seriously consider the prospect of delivering these lectures. And what could be more intimidating than to stand, metaphorically speaking, opposite such an array of extraordinary scholars and contemplate how in the world one was going to bring something worthy to this lecture series? One obvious ploy would be to concentrate on epigraphic and archaeological evidence that postdates the lifetimes of most of these scholars. Yet in my experience, even when new evidence appears, as soon as one seeks to integrate that with what is already known, one finds scholars of the past two or three centuries who have already dealt, in some fashion, with many of the same problems raised by the new data.

One field, however, which most of these scholars neglected to exploit in seeking to understand the Iranian evidence, is social anthropology. Thus, it gradually dawned on me that a diachronic perspective on issues associated with kinship, broadly speaking, was something that might be worth pursuing. Moreover, as a refugee from American anthropological archaeology, I was particularly attracted to issues of kinship. For all of the rhetoric of this field, there is often precious little anthropology, in the sense of classical subjects like kinship, in what American students are taught under the rubric of anthropological archaeology. Certainly, my own teachers had no interest in demonstrating how we might deploy the voluminous literature on kinship from social anthropology to better understand societies of the prehistoric or early historic past. Yet in my reading of the epigraphic and literary evidence pertaining to ancient Iran, I had on many occasions encountered issues that seemed ripe for elucidation using anthropological sources. Once I had decided on this course, it remained only for me to identify a suitable number of instances where this was the case and to stitch them together into five lectures. My choice of topics was highly idiosyncratic, but, first and foremost, they were ones in which I was myself interested.

The printed form of my Yarshater Lectures differs from the spoken form only in the insertion of a few more references, some rewriting, and the removal of quotations in French and German originally contained in the footnotes. These lectures certainly never pretended to be the last word on ancient Iranian kinship and social organization, but I hope that, by their example, whether as something to follow or as a subject for criticism, they will stimulate others to undertake further studies of this kind and thereby advance our understanding of Iran's past, in all its complexity, messiness, obscurity, and vibrancy, using insights gained by generations of anthropologists and historians. I am only too aware of the deficiencies in my own preparation for this sort of work, whether on an anthropological, historical, or philological level. But to paraphrase the Enlightenment scholar Jean Hardouin, I didn't get into this business just to say what others had already said before me (see Grafton 1999, 264n95).

1

Money Is to the West What Kinship Is to the Rest

I chose to focus on kinship and social organization in the Yarshater Lectures because I am fundamentally interested in the interactions of people in antiquity, much more so than in the plans of their houses or the temperature at which their pottery was fired. To be sure, there is a considerable body of studies that examines individuals in relation to Elamite law;[1] the institution of levirate marriage;[2] the sister's son in Elamite royal titulature and succession;[3] matrilinearity in Elam;[4] the Achaemenid tribes;[5] Achaemenid, Parthian, and Sasanian noble families;[6] the social and economic position of women;[7] marriage in Iranian late antiquity;[8] and the question of incest and close-kin marriage more generally.[9] I will touch on many of these topics because there is yet more to be said on them. Studies explicitly devoted to kinship systems, in contrast, are notably few and far between.[10] Yet, as the American anthropologist Marshall Sahlins observed in 1976, "money is to the West what kinship is to the Rest."[11] Even though this was a very glib,

1. See, e.g., Cuq 1931; Koschaker 1932, 1934, 1935a, 1935b, 1936b, 1941; Scheil 1939; Klíma 1963; Korošec 1964; Oers 2013; Badamchi 2018a, 2018b, 2019.
2. Yusifov 1974; Grillot 1988.
3. Glassner 1994; Quintana 2010; Potts 2018.
4. König 1926a; Koschaker 1933; van Soldt 1990.
5. Von Gall 1972; Briant 1990.
6. Neuhaus 1902; Christensen 1907, 1936; König 1924, 1926b; Herzfeld 1937; Jones 1996; Pourshariati 2008; Maksymiuk 2015; Hyland 2018; Orlov 2018.
7. Keiper 1879; Neuhaus 1902; Sancisi-Weerdenburg 1983; Larson 2006; Brosius 2010; Carter 2014; Matsushima 2016.
8. Gray 1915; Hjerrild 2003; Macuch 2007; Daryaee 2013.
9. Sanjana 1888; Cumont 1924; König 1964; Bigwood 2009; Frandsen 2009; Macuch 2010; Skjærvø 2013.
10. Perikhanian 1970; Herrenschmidt 1987; Macuch 2003, 2017.
11. Sahlins 1976, 216.

almost tongue-in-cheek, throwaway line, Sahlins's observation encapsulates the widely perceived difference in the standing of kinship in Western vs. non-Western societies and the underlying assumption, whether justified or not, that so-called "traditional" societies are more tightly bound by ties of kinship than Western, industrialized ones. Although I think this dichotomy is far too reductionist, I am not concerned here with modern social formations but with ancient Iranian ones.

SOME PRELIMINARY THOUGHTS AND CLARIFICATIONS

Traditionally, the study of kinship has been the domain of social anthropologists and sociologists who, unlike archaeologists and ancient historians, can actually interview informants. Kinship is far more deceptive than it might seem at first glance, for it is less about determining the identities of an individual's biological relationships than it is about revealing and appreciating socially constructed ones. As A. R. Radcliffe-Brown noted in 1950, "Two persons who are kin are related in one or other of two ways: either one is descended from the other, or they are both descended from a common ancestor." But descent is first and foremost "the social relationship of parents and children, not . . . the physical relation."[12] The impossibility of speaking to those whose kinship categories and systems we might wish to study has undoubtedly dissuaded many historians, philologists, and archaeologists from devoting much time to the topic. Yet there is plenty of evidence in the ancient sources of kinship relations in different ancient Iranian settings, as I will show, and this evidence makes sense only when it is treated like any other body of ethnographic data and interpreted in light of the innumerable anthropological studies that have been published in the course of the past 150 years, notwithstanding the objections of some scholars in the past who explicitly and almost proudly avowed an unwillingness to consult relevant anthropological literature for insights into ancient kinship systems. To cite just one example here: in 1926, a year in which the likes of Ruth Benedict, Franz Boas, R. B. Dixon, Melville J. Herskovits, Alfred L. Kroeber, Ralph Linton, Robert H. Lowie, Bronislaw Malinowski, Margaret Mead, Elsie Clews Parsons, A. R. Radcliffe-Brown, and a host of other extraordinarily important social anthropologists were active, Friedrich Wilhelm König (1897–1972; fig. 1) had the temerity to proudly declare, in a study of alleged Elamite matrilinearity, that he had intentionally resisted any impulse to draw ethnographic parallels with other cultures that might bear on the issue, for he believed it necessary to first extract everything that the Elamite "sources" had to offer. Then, and only then, when his conclusions were firmly based on the Elamite evidence, could he and should he present comparisons with other cultures that, he did not doubt, would cast matters in a different light. To do otherwise, he believed, would only

---

12. Radcliffe-Brown and Forde 1950, 13.

FIGURE 1. Friedrich
Wilhelm König.
Photographer
unknown. Archive
of the University of
Vienna, 106.1.2650.

prejudice his understanding of the Elamite evidence.[13] It is unfortunate, however, that despite his recognition of the potential importance of ethnographic studies to his own work, König never moved beyond the initial study of the Elamite source material to actually test his conclusions against the abundant anthropological and, in this case, literary analyses of scholars studying precisely the same phenomenon in various times and places.

Notwithstanding the reluctance of König and others of his ilk to engage with the anthropological literature in seeking to understand kin relations in ancient Iran, it should be obvious that people are the actors in history, and we don't really need the prosopographical studies of ancient historians, the multiple career-line analyses of sociologists, or the collective biographies of modern historians to validate

13. König 1926a, 529.

this premise.[14] Nor should it be the case that the consultation of comparable evidence from other times and places necessarily "corrupts" one's understanding of a particular historical phenomenon. This is tantamount to ignoring all precedents pertaining to a given law in legal or judicial practice. In fact, I cannot think of a situation in which we *shouldn't* apply exactly the *opposite* approach and scour the literature for similar expressions of a particular social practice, making every effort to understand it to the best of our abilities.

A further problem is endemic to the study of the ancient world. Because archaeologists and art historians tend to study material culture, and philologists tend to study literary and epigraphic sources, things like ceramic shapes and decoration, architecture, iconography, grammar, phonology, and loanwords often assume lives of their own and become, as objects of study, ends in themselves, leaving little time or space to draw conclusions about the people who created them. Similarly, the nature of the available ancient written sources in and about Iran means that, although they might wish it were not the case, ancient Near Eastern historians have often, *faute de mieux*, given military, political, and religious history priority over other fields. There are, of course, exceptions. Some economic historians have been at pains to stress the importance of family relationships in trading concerns, for example.[15] Yet, by and large, these sorts of studies are few and far between, and the decision to devote the Yarshater Lectures to kinship and society is a reflection of my very basic desire to get at the people who made the artifacts and who used the loanwords that we study—not necessarily as individual actors but as members of kinship units or social groups. This is what primarily motivates me to examine Iranian archaeology and history in the light of kinship and modes of social organization.

In prioritizing the people behind the artifacts, the kinship system behind the stele, or the society behind the archive, I am only doing what others have long advocated. For example, in his obituary of the Australian prehistorian Vere Gordon Childe, Robert J. Braidwood famously wrote more than sixty years ago, "Although Childe loved the artifacts he could understand, he never forgot the

---

14. Stone 1972, 46.

15. For a later but well-illustrated example, see Baladouni and Makepeace (1998, xxxiv):

> As opposed to the single, large, hierarchically organized joint-stock company, such as the English East India Company, the Armenian trading house was a network or alliance of organizations centered around a notable merchant, the khoja, who was at once business financier and entrepreneur. These widely spread but highly interrelated individual enterprises operated under an ethos of trust. Trust, and the shared moral and ethical norms underlying it, helped the Armenian trading houses to avoid the relatively rigid and costly operation of the hierarchic system of organization practiced by the English. Seen in this light, trust served as a human capital, but one that could not be acquired through a rational investment decision. It accrued to the Armenian merchant community as a result of their collective sociopolitical experiences over many generations. Based on family kinship and trusted fellow countrymen, the Armenian trading house did, indeed, rely on trust as its principal means of organization and control.

'Indian behind the artifact' and scolded his colleagues roundly if they did: e.g., 'Menghin insists so strongly on an axe as an expression of a historical tradition that the reader may forget that it is an implement for felling trees.'"[16] Actually, Braidwood's choice of this quotation was perhaps maladroit, for it would seem to warn against forgetting the functional, technical purpose of an artifact rather than the social context in which it was manufactured or its human maker. In any case, for the Austrian prehistorian Oswald Menghin's name here, one could easily substitute those of a multitude of archaeologists and art historians specializing in ancient Iran who, like Childe, "love" their cylinder seals, ceramics, rock reliefs, silver vessels, statuary, and inscriptions but, like Menghin, often ignore the people who fashioned or used them. By contrast, in the words of the Michigan anthropological archaeologist Kent Flannery, "the process theorist is not ultimately concerned with 'the Indian behind the artifact' but rather with the system behind both the Indian and the artifact."[17] To be very clear, nobody who has ever read a word I have written would classify me as a "process theorist," but I am interested in systems, albeit social rather than processual ones. But let us also be realistic: we are, after all, dealing with periods, the most recent of which is separated from our own time by over a millennium. Therefore, what we can expect to reveal, at the level of kinship and social organization, is necessarily fragmentary and shadowy—bits of a web of social relations rather than links in a well-preserved chain of kinship relations.

What I attempt in this volume might be characterized as historical anthropology, anthropological history,[18] or "retrospective ethnography," although since Charles Tilly characterized this last approach as one that seeks "to recreate crucial situations of the past as a thoughtful participant-observer would have experienced them,"[19] then it is clear that my own endeavor is nothing of the kind. Rather, my aim is to highlight those kinship, familial, and social structures, however poorly they may be represented in the written and archaeological record, that have tended to be sidelined or, if acknowledged at all, misunderstood, in previous studies of ancient Iran. Before continuing any further, however, a few words about the scope and chronology of this work are in order.

Iran is much more than a toponym. As Gherardo Gnoli showed so eloquently more than thirty years ago, Iran is, first and foremost, an idea.[20] No matter how much one parses the nomenclature of the Elamite, Achaemenid, and Sasanian royal inscriptions, or the classical sources on Persia, *Iran* remains an utterly anachronistic term in the discussion of any period prior to the appearance of the Achaemenid Empire in the mid-first millennium BC. Mesopotamian cuneiform sources abound in toponyms east of the Tigris, and while only a relatively small

16. Braidwood 1958, 734.
17. Flannery 1967, 120.
18. For these two terms see, e.g., Kalb et al. 1996.
19. Tilly 1984, 380.
20. Gnoli 1989.

number of these can be located with confidence, they leave us in no doubt that the area occupied today by the Islamic Republic of Iran was widely populated, culturally diverse, and anything but unified. To be sure, some regions were larger and more densely inhabited than others, but the only thing they have in common with Iran as we know it is their location east of the Tigris; north of the Persian Gulf and Arabian Sea; south of the Caucasus, the Caspian Sea, and the plains of Turkmenistan; and west of the mountains of Afghanistan and eastern Baluchistan. In other words, to use the term *Iranian* when discussing the archaeology and early history of the regions falling within the boundaries of modern Iran is to adopt a convention, and an anachronistic one at that. No Marhašian prince of the third millennium BC, Elamite scribe of the second millennium BC, or Median chieftain of the first millennium would have understood the term *Iran*. When, therefore, archaeologists and historians categorize a particular site and its finds, or a particular region, as "Iranian," this reflects an underlying assumption about what may or may not be included under this rubric, which almost always reflects the modern boundaries of the nation-state of Iran rather than any form of past cultural unity. Yet so ingrained have those boundaries become in our conception of Iran since the early nineteenth century that it is inordinately difficult to escape their strictures. Chronologically, therefore, all periods prior to the appearance of the first individuals in cuneiform sources with etymologically Iranian names can be considered pre-Iranian. Yet Iranian archaeology, as it has developed over more than a century, has appropriated the prehistoric, pre-Iranian, and non-Iranian Paleolithic, Neolithic, Chalcolithic, Bronze and Iron Age assemblages from sites across Azerbaijan, Kurdistan, Luristan, Khuzestan, Fars, Kerman, Baluchistan, Khorasan, the Central Plateau, and the circum-Caspian provinces, within the boundaries of modern Iran, deeming them the subjects of Iranian archaeology and ancient history. One may well ask, though, in what sense the Neolithic levels at Ganj Dareh in Luristan or the Bronze Age levels at Konar Sandal South in Jiroft are "Iranian"? The short answer to this question is "in no sense." We are fully justified in designating the totality of the prehistory of the Iranian plateau and its immediately adjacent lands West Asian or ancient Near Eastern, but to call it Iranian is to make a leap of faith and to impose a much later concept on sites and finds dating to periods in which the concept of Iranianness did not yet exist. Thus, by this definition, at least half of the subject matter I deal with in the pages that follow, concerning prehistoric and Elamite evidence, must be classified as "pre-Iranian."

The focus here on aspects of kinship that, in an Iranian context, have been understudied and often misunderstood also deserves a few words of further explanation. *Kinship* is a venerable term in anthropology and ethnology, and it has a tendency to conjure up "traditional," "primitive," or "tribal" societies—all deeply flawed terms—which we somehow know differed from complex agricultural and urban societies. *Kinship* triggers in some an expectation that the societies in which it is most important have a seemingly endless array of terms for mother's brother's sister's sons, and so forth. Kinship, visualized and concretized as a series of diagrams of marriage patterns, descent groups, and moieties, was dear to the hearts of many a Victorian and early twentieth-century scholar. Yet kinship is just as much with us today as it was with our ancestors. It constitutes a lens through which societies can be studied, and it will be the principal arc running through this book. This is not to say that competing forms of allegiance and group membership that crosscut biologically or socially based units and were not strictly based on kin relations haven't also played their part in human history or that all collective action in the societies examined here was based on kinship.[21] But it is important to move beyond simple characterizations of kinship ties as the glue that bound premodern societies together and to seek to understand those specific situations and institutions alluded to in ancient sources that have too often, in previous scholarship, been treated as aberrations largely because of an ignorance of comparative cases from later periods and other cultures around the world.

This study was never intended, however, to present a catalogue of kinship terms in Elamite, Old Persian, and Middle Persian, along the lines of Oswald Szemerényi's 1977 monograph on Indo-European kinship terminology[22] or R. S. P. Beekes's detailed analysis of terms for uncle and nephew in the Indo-European and proto-Indo-European languages.[23] Instead, I have tried to identify cases that illustrate a particular principle recognized in the anthropology of kinship but that has been overlooked or misunderstood. Some of these cases are attested only once in our admittedly fragmentary source material from the past. Others occur repeatedly, suggesting a pattern of kin-related practice that, far from unique, is attested in other cultures around the world as well, even if this has not always been appreciated. The scope ranges from prehistory, when the evidence is certainly sparse and always equivocal as well as controversial, to late antiquity.

To begin with, however, it may be helpful to clarify certain fundamental concepts that are frequently confused as they feature in subsequent chapters. At the heart of what David Schneider termed "the universe of kinship"[24] are two concepts: filiation and descent. Although often used interchangeably, these terms are not synonymous and are often used incorrectly in the historical literature. While the *Oxford English Dictionary* defines *filiation* as the "fact of being the child of a specified parent," filiation is necessarily bilateral or, as some scholars prefer to say, equilateral. As the British anthropologist Meyer Fortes noted more than

21. Similarly, in the case of Merovingian Franconia (Franken), White (2005, 86), for example, stressed that "in feuds waged by kings and nobles . . . pre-existing family groups did not spontaneously organize themselves to avenge injuries against one of their members. . . . Instead, feuds were occasions for constituting groups of kin to achieve multiple political purposes."

22. Szemerényi 1977. For a brief survey of kinship terms in New Persian see Bateni 1973.

23. Beekes 1976.

24. Schneider 1967, 65.

sixty years ago, filiation "is essentially the bond between successive generations."[25] *Descent*, however, as Fortes stressed, "can be defined as a genealogical connexion recognized between a person and any of his ancestors or ancestresses." Filiation and descent, he went on to stress, are "two analytically distinct institutions."[26]

In surveying the literature, we find it clear that many French- and German-speaking authors have not observed the strict distinction between filiation and descent favored by Anglophone anthropologists. The use of *filiation* when *descent* is in fact meant typifies exactly what Edmund Leach tried to clarify in a paper addressing Claude Lévi-Strauss's use of *filiation* rather than *descendance*.[27] The same pattern can be observed in the works of some Assyriologists, who have been known to use *filiation* synonymously with or in place of *descent*, as understood in the Anglophone anthropological literature, when in fact German *Filiation* should be distinguished from *Deszendenz*.[28]

The difference between these two terms is, moreover, extremely important. As Schneider emphasized, "Filiation originates in the domestic domain, descent in the politico-jural domain." Descent "has to do with a category of culturally differentiated statuses," some of which "are abstracted from a genealogical mesh or a universe of kinsmen . . . defined by a particular culture, and constituted as a single, conceptual category."[29] In Marshall Sahlins's words, "Descent is not recruitment but arrangement and alignment, in the first place a principle of political design, exercising arbitrary constraints on the suppositions of ancestry."[30] Descent may be unilineal and either patrilineal or matrilineal—that is, determined through the line of male or female ancestors—or it may be bilineal/bilateral—that is, determined through both ancestral lines. In questions of succession and inheritance, Fortes noted, descent "establishes what might be called a right to a place in the queue of potential successors."[31]

But we would also do well to bear in mind what Sahlins wrote more than fifty years ago:

---

25. Fortes 1959, 206.

26. Fortes 1959, 206.

27. Leach 1977.

28. Thus, speaking of a sequence of ancestors, rather than just ego's parent(s), Paulus (2013, 432) wrote of the *Filiation* of a series of Elamite kings, where, in fact, the German term *Deszendenz* (descent) is meant. Similarly, when Paulus referred to gaps in the filiation of Elamite rulers mentioned in the so-called Berlin Letter, it is important to note that, by definition, more than one gap, or two if the names of both parents are expected, necessarily implies descent, over multiple generations, as opposed to filiation, which concerns only ego and his/her parent(s). When Paulus says that the Berlin Letter (about which more below) invokes filiation as an argument for legitimate rights to succession to the throne, she clearly meant descent in the Anglo-American anthropological sense of the term. See Paulus 2013, 431.

29. Schneider 1967, 65.

30. Sahlins 1965, 104–6.

31. Fortes 1959, 208.

In major territorial descent groups, there is no particular relation between the descent ideology and group composition. . . . The ideology of descent has a career of
its own, largely independent of internal contradictions in recruitment. . . . Facts
of life overcome norms of membership. And if the facts be known, the ancestry
is mixed. . . . Purity of lineage has been undone. . . . Therefore, a serious objection is
in order to the popular tactic of perceiving structural principle ("jural rule") as the
outcome of how people are associated on the ground and in fact. In the conventional
wisdom, structure is the precipitate of practice. . . . But immediately we shift our
sights to the major descent system, the received wisdom falls to the ground.[32]

This perspective will be helpful when we turn to the question of matrilinearity in
ancient Iran, specifically in Elam, a topic on which simplistic conclusions have frequently been drawn based on evidence that, instead of testifying to the uniqueness
of Elamite social structure, simply needs to be understood in light of comparative
evidence from around the world.

One aspect of kinship systems that has gone largely unrecognized in most studies of Elamite, Achaemenid, Arsacid, and Sasanian society is the very important
distinction between what Lewis Henry Morgan (1818–81) termed classificatory vs.
descriptive kinship terminology. Although a voluminous body of literature, much
of it critical, has sprung up since the nineteenth century on the validity of this distinction, its fundamental utility remains, as argued cogently by Leslie White and
Meyer Fortes,[33] among others. To put it simply, classificatory relations are socially,
not biologically, defined. As Elman Service emphasized sixty years ago, "no one
has succeeded in showing that there is, in fact, a simple direct correlation between
an actual genealogical form of a society and a particular kind of kinship terminology." Moreover, paraphrasing Radcliffe-Brown, Service observed, "kinship terms
are used in address and reference as denotative of social positions relevant to inter-
personal conduct. They are, therefore, a form of status terminology"[34] and are not
always to be taken literally in the sense of biological relations between parents,
children, siblings, parents' siblings, and so forth. In other words, in classificatory
systems, fathers, mothers, sisters, brothers, aunts, and uncles are socially, not biologically, defined. As Morgan noted in describing the Malayan system, "my father's
brother is my father; his son and daughter are my brother and sister . . . and I
apply to them the same terms I do to my own brothers and sisters. . . . My father's
sister, in like manner, is my mother; her children are my brothers and sisters. . . .
My mother's brother is my father; and his children and descendants follow in the
same relationships as in the previous cases."[35] To cite another example, among
the Tallensi of northern Ghana, as Jack Goody noted, where "'sister' can refer to

32. Sahlins 1965, 104–6.
33. White 1958; Fortes 1969, 20–21.
34. Service 1960, 750.
35. Morgan 1868, 444–45.

clan females as a whole," the rule of exogamy is so strong that a taboo exists against marrying even distantly related classificatory "sisters."[36]

As demonstrated below, the distinction between biological and socially con-stituted parents and siblings, or members of different generations more broadly, has enormous implications for our understanding of many situations attested in ancient sources. Ignorant of the reality and significance of classificatory kinship systems, Western commentators have often naively assumed that every reference to a father, mother, brother, or sister implies the narrow, biological definition of such terms, as it would, generally speaking, apply in modern Western societies. Once that simplistic equivalence is stripped away, however, many problems that have plagued scholars for centuries can be resolved, such as the case of the Elamite king Hutelutuš-Inšušinak (c. 1120 BC), who refers to himself as the "son" of three different ancestors. In the same way, when descent is viewed as an organizing principle, rather than the projection of a biological diagram, then the question is not whether a family tree is fabricated or falsified, a charge that has sometimes been leveled at certain ancient Iranian rulers, nor is the issue at stake "genealogical amnesia" vs. accurate recording. Rather, descent is a blueprint of recruitment and inclusion, as Sahlins stressed. We should keep this perspective in mind when we look at some of the Elamite and Old Persian evidence, in particular, for, as Fortes pointed out, paraphrasing Bronislaw Malinowski, "a genealogy is, in fact . . . a legal charter and not an historical record."[37] This sounds like a sentiment with which Darius I would have concurred.

Turning now to preferential marriage patterns, these are often intimately linked to kinship and feature in several of the chapters herein. A favorite topic of anthro-pologists all over the world, like kinship studies in general, preferential marriage patterns have received less attention in the study of Near Eastern antiquity, except, it seems, when it comes to incest or so-called next-of-kin marriages. Two forms of preferential marriage, so-called cross-cousin and parallel-cousin marriage, have generated an enormous body of literature since the nineteenth century. Cross-cousins, a term coined by E. B. Tylor (1832–1917),[38] are the children of siblings of the opposite sex (that is, brothers and sisters), whereas parallel-cousins are the children of siblings of the same sex (that is, of a set of brothers or a set of sisters). This classification is linked to the concept of the "moiety," since cross-cousins are by definition members of opposite halves or moieties of a group, whereas parallel-cousins, like siblings, are always members of the same half.[39] For Tylor, "cross-cousin marriage is part and parcel of exogamy," and exogamy is the surest

---

36. Goody 1956, 302.
37. Fortes 1953, 27–28.
38. Tylor 1889, 263. Cf. Crawley 1907.
39. Urban 1996, 100.

means of building alliances for social groups faced with "the simple practical alternative between marrying-out and being killed out."[40]

Marriage preferences, however, are rarely strictly binary. Adam Kuper noted what all of us have probably observed in our own social circles: "Sustained alliances between a few families in the same ecological niche gave the members of these clans a powerful competitive advantage."[41] Yet as Malinowski's South African student Isaac Schapera observed in the case of the Tswana of Botswana, while cross-cousin marriage was preferred, any cousin would do, and although matrilateral cross-cousin marriage was common throughout Tswana society, Tswana nobles opted when possible for patrilateral parallel-cousin marriage—that is, with the father's brother's daughter. As Kuper wrote, "In both cases, the reason was very similar. Men tried to reinforce relationships with powerful kin. For a commoner, these were often mothers' brothers. For a noble, the best-placed relatives would be fathers' brothers."[42] In fact, there is perhaps no better illustration of this, as Kuper pointed out, than the Rothschild family, who, from 1824 to 1877, witnessed the marriages of thirty-six patrilineal descendants of the *pater familias* Mayer Amschel Rothschild, thirty of which involved cousins and twenty-eight of which were first and second cousins. "First or second cousins related through the male line only."[43] This means that a staggering 78 percent of those marriages involved parallel-cousins.

THE NEXT STEP

The topics just adduced all feature in the following chapters, where I discuss a range of issues extending from succession and endogamy to dowry, brideprice, residence, the definition of tribe, patronymics, the avunculate, the levirate, and feudalism. As noted above, the lectures on which this text is based were never envisioned as a comprehensive presentation of kinship terms, let alone an exhaustive inventory of all kin-related data in ancient Iran. Rather, the aim was to highlight instances in the sources where our understanding can be deepened by drawing on insights from the work of some of the giants of social anthropology, as well as data from non-Iranian historical and literary studies. This attempt—for it is nothing more than that—should not be seen as an effort to privilege the data or conclusions of anthropology over those of the diverse branches of ancient Iranian studies. Nor is it a thought experiment. In deploying insights from anthropology,

---

40. Tylor 1889, 265, 267. In Fredrik Barth's opinion, "This fact of exogamy has important implications, e.g. for the development of dispersed clans and normalizing of a 'daughter's son' relationship as a mechanism for grafting foreign lineages to the dominant lineage of an area" (Barth 1986, 389).

41. Kuper 2008, 721.

42. Kuper 2008, 727.

43. Kuper 2008, 728.

I simply mean to open the way toward a better understanding of some of the Iranian data that may have gone unnoticed, underappreciated, or simply misunderstood over the years and to broaden the perspectives of historians, philologists, and archaeologists for whom the social fabric of past societies has, at times, been given less emphasis than it deserves.

2

Aspects of Kinship in Iranian Prehistory

As noted above, whereas social anthropologists can interview their informants, archaeologists and ancient historians cannot. In one respect, this is an obvious disadvantage. In another sense, however, it leaves the door wide open for speculations that can be difficult to refute, debunk, or at least be shown to be implausible, once enshrined in the literature. Given the absence of written sources, any reconstruction of the social organization of the earliest sedentary societies in the Near East, particularly in Iran, is always going to be speculative. Even at a biological level, assuming human skeletal remains from cemeteries could be recovered from which DNA could be extracted, or teeth were excavated which preserved epigenetic traits to establish kinship,[1] we might be in a position to tell that people were related, but this is to be expected in any relatively small community, and such analyses would not tell us *how* they were related or what kind of kinship patterns were present. Although Ernst Herzfeld claimed that "Back to prehistoric times goes the fourfold graduation of Iranian social order into *nmāna-* 'house,' *vis-* 'clan,' *zantu-* 'tribe,' and *dahyū-* 'people,'"[2] we have no way of verifying this claim and, a priori, it seems more likely that the pre- or non-Iranian groups inhabiting Iran in prehistory were not organized according to the same principles as later Iranians were, at least according to the Avesta. Nevertheless, some categories of finds from Neolithic and Chalcolithic contexts (c. 8000–3500 BC) have been adduced in discussions of society and social relations, albeit in a rather oblique fashion, and these provide us with our first material for examination here.

---

1. See, e.g., Alt and Vach 1991 for the method. For an illustration of the study of epigenetic traits to identify relatedness among individuals in a Bronze Age collective burial in the Oman peninsula, see Alt et al. 1995.

2. Herzfeld 1937, 937.

APPROACHING THE SOCIAL ASPECT OF CERAMICS

Nonarchaeologists who have even a passing acquaintance with Near Eastern archaeological literature dealing with some portion of the last eight or nine thousand years are probably aware of the outsized significance of ceramics in the study of the ancient Near East. The reduction of a mass of ceramic data, often comprising thousands and thousands of broken pieces of pottery, coupled with tens of thousands of both qualitative and quantitative observations on them, into a coherent typology of forms and decorations that may be taken as the ceramic signature of a site, and then compared with the ceramic signatures of other sites, is among the primary aims of such studies. To say that work like this is labor-intensive, often tedious, and frequently an end in itself is an understatement.

The difficulty, of course, arises in attempting to convert typological data into social insights. When I was a student, a powerful reaction set in against the notion, often derided as hopelessly simplistic, that pots equal people—in other words, that the ceramic assemblage of a site, as a cultural signature, characterized the site's inhabitants and could be used to identify those people and chart their interactions, trade, conquests, and movements through space and time. Deploying a sort of neo-Boasian logic, it was argued that material culture, language, and "race," by which we might today say biological group affinity, varied independently of each other.[3] Hence, people who belonged to linguistically and biologically different groups, might still use similar material culture. Conversely, they might belong to the same biological or linguistic group but use different sorts of material culture. The warning was, therefore, clear: do not assume that a pottery style or assemblage, by which we understand the totality of forms, decorative modes, and functional categories in a site, stratigraphic unit, or region, was necessarily coterminous with a discrete human social unit, whether a small village, a federation of clans and families, or an entire nation.

Despite this sort of admonition, however, archaeologists have often found it almost impossible to decouple a ceramic style or its regional distribution at a series of contemporary sites, within a circumscribed area, from the notion of a social group. For example, it may be tempting to conflate so-called Lapui pottery, a fourth-millennium BC assemblage first identified on the Marv Dasht plain,[4] with a concrete ancient community, even if modern archaeologists no longer use labels based on the chief characteristic of the pottery of a region in a particular period, like "the buff-ware culture," or the "gray-ware culture." Nor would most archaeologists today interpret the diverse wares present at a single site as evidence of distinct "cultures." In the past, however, they did just that. For example, Donald E. McCown (1910–85) suggested in 1942 that the "light-toned pottery" and

3. See, e.g., Boas 1940.
4. Sumner 1988.

the "red ware" of Tappeh Sialk I "typify two different cultures."[5] In some cases, such pseudosocial, group identifications were further refined and conceptualized, for example, as tribes or part of a confederation of tribes, without even defining just what a tribe is.[6] More commonly, however, the explicit characterization of a ceramically-defined "group" as a band, lineage, tribe, clan, community, people, and so forth is left unstated, even when the identification of a ceramic assemblage or stylistic horizon with some form of human group is implicit.

In contrast, technological ascriptions are entirely justifiable, but whether or not they translate into demographic "signatures" is another matter altogether. Thus, for example, in 1965, when the late Robert H. Dyson Jr. identified an early "software horizon" in Iran, he correctly highlighted the widespread occurrence of a shared technology of pottery vessel construction by hand and of firing at low temperatures,[7] a technology later investigated by Pamela Vandiver, who called it "sequential slab construction" because of the use of individual slabs of clay to build up the body of a vessel.[8] Although Dyson scrupulously avoided conflating this technocomplex with a "people," some scholars discuss ceramic assemblages, even such technologically defined types, as if they were living and breathing organisms rather than expressions of particular makers and diverse human groups employing a common technology. A particularly striking example of this is found in the work of Donald E. McCown. When discussing period I4 at Tappeh Sialk, for example, he wrote that "the red-ware culture began to influence the light-ware culture of Siyalk I . . . [and] by the time of Siyalk II the red-ware culture was predominant and had eliminated the use of light ware."[9] In more recent scholarship, too, an organismic analogy is sometimes implicit. Assemblages and styles may stand isolated; they may integrate; they may hybridize, as if a process of ceramic natural selection were at work, an unseen hand shepherding this material along over centuries, even millennia. The fundamental difficulty, of course, is that archaeologists are often capable of identifying and describing phenomena for which they can offer no explanation. When explanations are proffered, however, it is incumbent on us to consider whether they are either necessary or sufficient.

Following a time-honored practice in North American archaeology, some ceramic assemblages, ware groups, or stylistic/decorative groups are named after so-called type sites—that is, the sites where they were first recorded, or where they were particularly well-represented, or after villages or towns close to those sites. This approach is not universal in Iran, but some American archaeologists have used it. These include Joseph Caldwell at Tal-e Iblis in Kerman province;[10] Robert

5. McCown 1942, 2.

6. On the tribe as a political construct see the discussion in chaps. 3 and 4 below.

7. Dyson 1965, 217.

8. Vandiver 1987.

9. McCown 1942, 2.

10. See, e.g., Caldwell (1967, 114) for types such as Bard Sir Painted, Iblis Plain, Lalehzar Coarse, etc.

H. Dyson Jr. at Hasanlu in the Urmia basin;[11] Frank Hole, Kent V. Flannery, and James Neely on the Deh Luran plain;[12] and William M. Sumner at Tal-e Malyan in the Marv Dasht plain of Fars. In the case of prehistoric Fars, for example, Sumner suggested that "the presence of Jari, Kutahi, Bizdan, and possibly local styles in Kazerun and Sarvestan implies a degree of cultural isolation in the plains of the valleys of Fars."[13] On the basis of later research by the Mamasani Archaeological Project, this view was queried by Lloyd Weeks and his coauthors, who pointed to the presence, at some sites in the area, of shells from the Persian Gulf, copper from the central Iranian plateau, obsidian from eastern Anatolia and southern Armenia, and bitumen from Khuzestan or Iraq—all of which speaks against the notion of cultural isolation.[14] Moreover, they also stressed the fact that Kutahi ware has been found near Shiraz, while Jalyan and Bizdan wares are attested in Fasa and Darab. This, too, suggests anything but cultural isolation. But there is a further line of inquiry raised by Sumner that I believe has been overlooked but may prove productive.

It is a widely held belief that before pottery manufacture became industrialized and potting became a full-time profession, it was situated physically in the individual households of families, what Max Weber called the *Hausgemeinschaft*,[15] where pottery was made by and for one or more household's own use. It need not follow, of course, that, on a technical level, each household potter used perceptibly different methods to fashion their pottery. On the contrary, at any given point in time, within one region, there was probably always broad uniformity in manufacturing technique, with some measure of personal idiosyncrasy, experimentation, or a desire to do things differently accounting for elements of regional variation. Decoration, of course, varied as well. Within a community, there may have been broad norms and mental templates on which potters based their designs, as well as variation that reflected individual tastes, artistic ability, physical coordination, and sensibility. Taken out of a community context, and compared with the products of another village or kin-group, pottery styles may have seemed even more distinctive and distinguishable, not because potters tried consciously to express their group identity but because the way they approached their work and the way in which they had been taught by their kith and kin combined to produce a distinctive potting signature. Hence, where different styles as defined by archaeologists appear alongside each other—for example, in the same archaeological stratum or series of strata at one site—I would interpret this not as a sign of isolation, as Sumner suggested, but of the colocation of divergent styles made by individual

---

11. See, e.g., Voigt and Dyson (1992, 174–75) for types such as Hajji Firuz Ware, Urmia Plain, Pisdeli Painted, etc.

12. See, e.g., Hole, Flannery, and Neely (1969, 116–22, 162–63) for types such as Jaffar Plain, Khazineh Red, Memeh red-on-red, and Bayat Red.

13. Sumner 1977, 303.

14. Weeks et al. 2006, 20.

15. Hellmann and Palyi 1923, 41.

potters in one community. The question is, what circumstances might lead to such a situation?

Obviously, barter or exchange is one mechanism that could effect a spread of stylistically distinctive pottery between communities, but in societies where goods produced in the household stayed, for the most part, in the household, the appearance of diverse styles in one and the same settlement might instead indicate the presence of individuals from different communities, not because of trade and exchange but because of marriage patterns. In other words, the practice of exogamy could create a situation in which diverse styles that show no apparent relation to each other appear alongside one another at an archaeological site.

Reinhard Bernbeck queried precisely this sort of hypothesis thirty years ago in his study of the Neolithic pottery from Qale Rostam in the Bakhtiyari mountains, near modern Lordegan. As Bernbeck pointed out, three assumptions prevailed in Americanist investigations of ceramic production and kinship: first, that ceramic production was, in most cases, a female activity;[16] second, that the crafts of pottery making and decoration were passed on from mother to daughter; and third, that a unified ceramic assemblage, with respect to form and decoration over time, implied that women (i.e., the makers of the pottery) remained in their original settlements after marriage and did not move to those of their husbands, if in fact exogamy was practiced. In other words, regardless of whether marriage was endogamous or exogamous, if stylistic continuity characterized a site over a period of decades or centuries, then residence was most probably matrilocal. To put it another way, the ceramic repertoire of the site was reproduced by female potters from generation to generation in the same locale.[17]

But for purposes of interrogating the more remote past, my concern is not so much whether pottery was made by men or women. Rather, the main issue is whether the ceramic assemblage of an archaeological site is stylistically, in form and decoration, relatively homogeneous—that is, whether or not the decorative patterns appear consistent within a particular design vocabulary. I raise this because the situation at Tol-e Nurabad in western Fars, c. 6000 BC, for example, evidences extreme variability (fig. 2).[18] There, pottery that is enormously diverse, from a decorative point of view, appears in the same stratigraphic and therefore chronological context.

Such a situation could suggest exogamy. On one hand, if men made the pottery, then this degree of diversity could imply that they went to live in the home villages or settlements of their wives—an exogamous, matrilocal residence pattern—bringing with them their own suite of decorative patterns, which they painted on pottery manufactured for household use. If, on the other hand, women made the

16. See Bernbeck 1989, 186. With respect to industrial-scale ceramic factories, in ancient Mesopotamia, where these are attested in a wealth of cuneiform sources from the last century of the third millennium BC (Ur III period), the potters were men. See, e.g., Waetzoldt 1970–71; Sallaberger 1996.

17. Bernbeck 1989, 188. Cf. Allen and Richardson 1971.

18. Weeks et al. 2006.

FIGURE 2. Painted Neolithic pottery from Tol-e Nurabad in Fars, Iran. TNP 1432 (left) and TNP 1480 (right). Photo by the author.

FIGURE 3. Painted Neolithic pottery sherd from Tol-e Nurabad in the hands of a modern archaeologist with a clay object that may have been used to apply pigment. Photo by the author.

pottery, as seems more likely based on ethnographic evidence from around the world, then the diversity seen at Tol-e Nurabad would imply that women went to the home villages of their husbands, continued to make pottery for their new households, and thereby introduced new decorative patterns (fig. 3). Marriage may therefore have been exogamous and residence patrilocal. We may not be able to determine whether residence in a given prehistoric situation was patrilocal or matrilocal, but the high degree of ceramic variation within an assemblage like that of Neolithic Tol-e Nurabad strongly suggests an exogamous marriage pattern.

In 1971, William Allen and James B. Richardson III argued that the determination of residence patterns from archaeological evidence was fraught with difficulty. Indeed, in discussing a Pacific example, they cited the case of two anthropologists studying the same community, and interviewing the same households, who came to diametrically opposed views on the question of whether residence in that community was patrilocal or ambilocal (i.e., mixed, in which some married couples resided matrilocally while others resided patrilocally).[19] They also stressed the enormous divergence between ideal norms—what people say they do—and what people actually do. They questioned "the assumption that one can recover any uniformly prescriptive or preferential rules of residence." In fact, they suggested that, "given the multiplicity of obstacles that confront . . . archaeologists in their attempts to make meaningful statements about prehistoric kinship systems, it seems justified to conclude that unless extremely detailed historic data exists, the analysis of kinship is best left to the ethnographer."[20] All of this should be heeded, and cautionary tales abound, but it is, at one level, irrelevant, in my opinion, since the degree of variation seen in an assemblage like Tol-e Nurabad is consistent with population admixture. So long as pottery production in the Neolithic was a household activity, exogamy seems likely to have played a role in the distribution of diverse ceramic styles within one community rather than aesthetic sensibilities that varied wildly from household to household or intervillage and interregional exchange.

In some situations, archaeologists working in Iran have suggested that some painted decorative styles represent "hybrids"—that is, a fusion of two distinct traditions. This has been suggested in the case of pottery recovered in Chalcolithic graves at Hakalan and Dum Gar Parchinah in the Pusht-e Kuh, Luristan. More precisely, it has been suggested that "the hybrid style of some painted pottery vessels, not found elsewhere, may not only be attributed to the practice of interregional marriages; assuming women were active in pottery production, it also fits nicely with the mobile characteristic of . . . migratory tribes."[21] Setting aside for the moment this reference to "migratory tribes," of which there is no evidence in this instance,[22] it is intriguing that, whereas I have just pointed to residence patterns and exogamy as mechanisms that could account for the appearance of utterly distinctive painted pottery types at a site, through the arrival of their makers, whether men or women, in the communities of their spouses, here hybridity is interpreted as a possible result of exogamy. Furthermore, it has been suggested

19. Allen and Richardson 1971: 44–45.
20. Allen and Richardson 1971, 45, 51.
21. Alizadeh 2008, 18.
22. Potts 2014, 16–20.

that "if women were active potters or pot painters in prehistory . . . interregional marriages in patrilocal societies certainly would lead to the spread of specific pottery styles that in the course of time would become either diluted or would undergo hybridization."[23] While this may, in theory, be possible, such an explanation would require that a potter from an outside community adopted some of the stylistic conventions of his or her new family or group and combined these with his or her own conventional patterns. Certainly in the case of Neolithic Tol-e Nurabad, hybridity is not the issue, but rather the colocation of completely different styles in one and the same stratigraphic level, suggesting that, if potters from outside communities changed their places of residence, they continued to make pottery as they had always done and did not fuse the styles of their new home with those of their traditional practice.

Regardless of how close to the mark or otherwise these speculations on ancient pottery production in Iran may be, we cannot escape one obdurate fact, namely, that the potters and painters of ancient Iranian ceramics will forever be anonymous. One qualification to this statement, however, is prompted by the widely documented, if far from universal, practice of inscribing or painting so-called potter's marks on pottery. Many years ago I undertook a study of the incised marks on pottery from Tappeh Yahya as part of my dissertation. Shortly after I published a paper on these,[24] another study appeared by the French prehistorian Geneviève Dollfus and the linguist Pierre Encrevé discussing painted potter's marks on fifth-millennium BC pottery from Tappehs Jaffarabad, Bendebal, and Jowi in Susiana.[25]

At the time, I was interested in the possibility that the potter's marks of Tappeh Yahya preserved some graphic similarities with so-called Proto-Elamite or Susa III writing, attested at Susa and elsewhere, including Tappeh Yahya, which were transmitted via Baluchistan to the Indus Valley, where similar signs were attested in the Harappan script.[26] This is not a suggestion to which I would adhere today; in fact, if I were to reanalyze the potter's marks of any ancient Iranian site now, I would work from considerably different premises.

Many scholars have assumed that pottery was marked by prehistoric potters prior to firing in communal kilns so that their products would be easily recognizable and retrievable. As a corollary, some scholars have suggested that marks made, whether painted or incised, after firing indicated ownership. In 1983, for example, the late K. C. Chang pointed out that, at several sites in China, certain potter's marks were specific to particular areas within a site, leading him to suggest that these were not the marks of potters but were rather "markers and emblems of families, lineages, clans, or divisions of these."[27] This is analogous to the *tamga*

---

23. Alizadeh 2006, 26n56.
24. Potts 1981.
25. Dollfus and Encrevé 1982.
26. See also Potts 1982.
27. Chang 1983, 85.

used much later by steppe groups and Iranians, a subject treated in the final chapter of this study. A somewhat similar explanation has been proposed for the marks on Susiana pottery published by Dollfus and Encrevé and attested at Choga Mish as well. Given that more than two hundred potter's marks were found at Choga Mish, it has been suggested that these were not the marks of individual potters but rather marks that "indicated household or corporate groups who either had their vessels baked in a common fire, or else identified their vessels in common storage facilities, of which there is no evidence."[28] This, however, seems highly unlikely. In this regard, it is interesting that, in a wide-ranging review of nonindustrial ceramic production around the world, the late Carol Kramer found that whereas "some potters use identification marks . . . even in the absence of such marks, potters can usually identify their own products and often those made by other potters in their community as well," while others "use identifying marks only when firing jointly with another potter."[29] Another type of marking, which probably did not obtain in ancient Iran, at least in the prehistoric era, was the marking of pottery with the name of a customer (i.e., a purchaser). This implies a market and professionalization of pottery manufacture that only came about much later in time.

EXOGAMY IN THE PREHISTORIC RECORD

We turn now to another way in which ceramics in ancient Iran have been interpreted. Exogamous marriage patterns have also been invoked to account for the geographical distribution of a single, largely homogenous and easily recognizable category of ceramics: the so-called Bakun A pottery. Named after the Chalcolithic site of Tal-e Bakun near Persepolis (fig. 4), investigated in the spring and summer of 1932 by Alexander Langsdorff and Donald E. McCown,[30] the Bakun A ceramic assemblage, dating to the early fifth millennium BC,[31] is dominated by a distinctive, well-fired, black-painted buffware. This, however, was not produced in individual households. Rather, it was made by highly skilled potters who had access to well-controlled kilns and were capable or replicating their products on a reliable basis. Although it has been suggested that "interregional marriages, an important factor in forging interregional alliances through kinship, could also be considered as a contributing factor in the spread of some classes of pottery,"[32] in the case of the very fine Bakun A pottery, its spatial distribution, according to one interpretation, corresponded to "the locations of summer/winter pastures of the tribes of Qashqai, Bakhtiari, Khamseh, Mamasani and Boyr-Ahmadi

---

28. Alizadeh 2008, 10.

29. Kramer 1985, 82.

30. Langsdorff and McCown 1942.

31. Some of the best-dated deposits with classic Bakun pottery were excavated at Tol-e Nurabad. These date to c. 4800–4000 cal. BC. See Weeks, Petrie, and Potts 2010, 257 and table 16.1.

32. Alizadeh 2006, 17.

FIGURE 4. Tal-e Bakun A. Photo courtesy of Parse-Pasargadae Foundation Archive, ICHHTO, Fars, Iran.

confederacies"; hence, Abbas Alizadeh argued that "nomadic tribes . . . dispersed Bakun A culture over vast areas."[33]

One wonders, of course, where these hypothetical nomads acquired the fine Bakun A-type pottery they are alleged to have carried with them all over Fars, since it has not been suggested that it was actually made by them. Nor is the use of pottery characteristic of the very nomadic groups cited as models for fifth-millennium behavior. The French anthropologist Jean-Pierre Digard, who lived with and wrote extensively on the Bakhtiyari, noted that they used only containers made from organic materials, such as wood, along with wool, skin, hair, and fleece, whereas pottery was "totally absent" in their lives.[34]

SOCIAL ENDOGAMY?

The architectural and glyptic record at Tal-e Bakun has also prompted some scholars to speculate on the practice of social endogamy at the site. It has been suggested that "a change in social structure that we can barely see archaeologically, i.e., a separation of kinship from economic and political considerations," occurred at the site, and that "the internally specialized nature of the settlement at Tall-e Bakun A and the system of control exercised by some to limit access to certain parts of the community is . . . indicative of the presence of at least two class-endogamous strata."[35] Furthermore, in an effort to interpret the presence of sealings produced

33. Alizadeh 1988, 28.
34. Digard 1975, 120.
35. Alizadeh 2006, 17.

by three different stamp seals in Building IV at the site, it has been argued that "since Tall-e Bakun A was a prehistoric society in which kinship ties may still have been strong enough to be a major factor in the workings of the socioeconomic organization, it can be postulated that Building IV belonged to a father, who carried Seal 1, and his two children, who carried Seals 3 and 5."[36] We have here a series of inferences that may be restated as follows: first, the social order at the site consisted of two strata that were "class-endogamous," by which one may assume that marriage was restricted to members of one's class and did not occur across the two hypothesized "classes" of Bakun A society; and second, seal impressions produced by three different stamp seals, found in one particular building, can be attributed to a male and two of his children, whether male or female.

With respect to the first of these inferences, social-class endogamy is a well-attested phenomenon. In his posthumously published *Wirtschaftsgeschichte*, Max Weber identified class endogamy—a situation in which daughters from élite clans married only their social equals—as one of the factors that contributed to the breakdown of the patriarchal *Hausgemeinschaft*.[37] More recently, as van Leeuwen and Maas noted, "social endogamy refers to marrying within the same class—and thus assumes the existence of a limited number of discrete classes—while social homogamy refers to marrying someone of approximately the same status—and thus assumes the existence of a continuous status scale."[38] One doesn't need to have seen *Downton Abbey* or read Anthony Trollope or Jane Austen to be able to conjure up many examples of both social endogamy and social homogamy. But as van Leeuwen and Maas correctly observed, the assumption of discrete classes is integral to the concept of social endogamy, and it surely stretches credulity to infer the existence of two social classes at Tal-e Bakun A simply because someone sealed off the door of a storage room, thereby implying that some individuals had access to its contents while others did not.

Equally suspect, moreover, is the above-cited inference about seal ownership. The assumption was based on the recovery of sixty-three door sealings in Building IV, the impressions of which were made by three different seals. Of these, Seal 1 accounted for thirty-six sealings, Seal 5 for fifteen, and Seal 3 for twelve.[39] Any inference about a potential familial relationship between the owners or, rather, users of these three seals must confront a significant chronological consideration. In fact, the recovery of these sealings in one archaeological "horizon" at Tal-e Bakun A by no means indicates that they were all produced and used contemporaneously, particularly as the horizon in question has been dated to a four-century-long

---

36. Alizadeh 2006, 88.

37. See Hellmann and Palyi 1923, 58: "Der Bruch erfolgte durch die ständische Endogamie, indem vornehme Sippen ihre Töchter nur an Gleichgestellte verheirateten."

38. Van Leeuwen and Maas 2005, 1.

39. Alizadeh 1988, table 1; Alizadeh 2006, table 31.

period, from 4500 to 4100 BC.[40] Thus, many alternative scenarios could be invoked to account for the presence of sealings from three different seals in one building (Building IV). The seals could have all belonged to one individual who, in the course of a lifetime spanning decades, used three different seals, either successively or concurrently. Alternatively, they could have belonged to three individuals, whether united by kinship ties or unrelated, who were responsible for the building in three successive centuries. Theoretically, ownership or stewardship of the building may have changed hands multiple times during the 400 year occupation of Tal-e Bakun A, and multiple generations may have separated the users of each seal. These are just a few of the considerations that must be considered in seeking to understand seal ownership at Tal-e Bakun.

NEOLOCAL RESIDENCE

In addition to patrilocal and matrilocal residence, another pattern not yet considered in this discussion is neolocal residence—that is, the situation in which a man and wife move away from their parental homes and natal villages and establish an entirely new residence. This raises an intriguing point about archaeological site formation that is often overlooked. Archaeologists are very familiar with the concept of virgin soil—that is, the ground surface on which the initial occupation of a settlement occurred—but we are not generally in the habit of considering the demographic implications of that first occupation of a site, which may in fact imply a neolocal residence pattern in the sense that the human actors involved had to have come from somewhere else before settling on virgin soil. The population implications are unclear, however, and need not necessarily reflect population growth and the fission of a preexisting settlement, with some inhabitants moving away to found a new one. As Arnold Wilson observed in 1908, "the Persian habit of deserting villages and houses, and of rebuilding houses, when necessary, upon new sites, is too well known to require mention."[41]

A new settlement or resettlement, of course, need not only occur at the start of a site's life. Archaeological sites are routinely abandoned, sometimes permanently, but often for an interval of time ranging from months or years to centuries or even millennia. The underlying causes of such periodic abandonments are many and varied, and in the premodern era we generally have few indicators, apart from signs of past earthquakes or paleoclimatic data suggesting drought, that would have induced the inhabitants of one site to leave it and establish residence elsewhere.[42] In the nineteenth-century literature, however, vivid descriptions of settlement abandonment caused by cholera epidemics, plague, war, drought, and

---

40. Alizadeh 2006, 5. Previously the Bakun A phase had been dated to 4100–3700 BC. See Alizadeh 1988, 17.

41. Wilson 1908, 157.

42. See, e.g., Berberian et al. 2012, 2014.

famine exist.[43] These phenomena undoubtedly played a role in the remote past as well, not only drastically reducing populations periodically but causing major demographic shifts as some groups left their homes to establish new ones from scratch, while others joined existing settlements, swelling their numbers, and still others resettled on top of previously abandoned, unoccupied settlements. Neolocal residence patterns probably lurk behind some of the frequent stratigraphic and architectural discontinuities observed by archaeologists, for instance in the case of architecture built on a completely different orientation to that beneath it following a period in which a site had lain abandoned.

DETECTING DOWRIES ARCHAEOLOGICALLY

A further, marriage- and hence kinship-related feature has also been invoked in discussing the prehistoric cemeteries of Hakalan and Dum Gar Parchinah excavated by the late Louis Vanden Berghe. In an effort to understand the distribution of diverse objects found in the tombs there, it has been suggested that "such objects (at least some of them) may have been part of the 'dowries' acquired through inter-regional marriages, an important factor in forging inter-regional alliances through kinship."[44] To the best of my knowledge, neither dowry nor brideprice have elsewhere been invoked as mechanisms that could account for the spatial distribution of material culture in ancient Iran, although they have been in Mesopotamia.[45] As such, these are interesting concepts to consider here.

"Dowry," as Jack Goody and Stanley Tambiah noted half a century ago, "can be seen as a type of pre-mortem inheritance to the bride."[46] A dowry was traditionally given from father to daughter, without intermediaries taking a share. The evolutionary anthropologist Laura Fortunato and her colleagues have noted that "in monogamous societies characterized by uneven resource distribution . . . parents can increase their inclusive fitness by securing a high-status husband for their daughters." As a result, "forms of female-biased parental investment such as dowry are more common in these societies than elsewhere."[47] Like bridewealth or brideprice—the transfer of wealth by the bridegroom and his family to the bride and her family—the movement of goods as dowry with a woman in a patrilocal situation could certainly, after a woman's death or the death of her descendants and heirs, result in the appearance of what might be considered foreign items, particularly jewelry (earrings, finger rings, or torques), in the grave.[48] But many items in ancient Mesopotamian dowries, on which we have written records from

43. See, e.g., Potts 2014, 305–7 with refs.
44. Alizadeh 2008, 18.
45. See, e.g., Brereton 2016, 204.
46. Goody 1973, 1.
47. Fortunato et al. 2006: 356.
48. Roth 1989/1990, 2, 17–19, 33.

the third through the first millennium BC, were made of perishable materials and, consequently, have left no trace archaeologically. These include various items of clothing and other textiles, leather bags, reed baskets, and animal-hide rugs, not to mention wooden tables, chairs, chests, beds, combs,[49] and spoons, as well as slaves and oil.[50] Moreover, in some cases land—a field or a date grove—constituted part of a bride's dowry.[51] In other cases, however, items that would have been useful, if not absolutely essential, seem never to have typically formed part of a woman's dowry. As Stephanie Dalley noted in discussing Old Babylonian dowries in Mesopotamia of early second-millennium BC date, "Although the basis of a dowry was to provide the needs of a domestic woman, none of these dowries include knives. . . . Mirrors also are not found. . . . A sieve . . . is not found. . . . Not every woman took spindles or a loom to the new house."[52]

In thinking about the archaeological correlates of dowries, however, we must remember that the diffusion of goods could also be effected in other ways. As the Dutch Assyriologist Marten Stol noted, "as early as the betrothal some or all of the dowry would be made over to the man,"[53] a practice that could result in the appearance of what were originally dowry objects in both male and female graves. Similarly, the law code known as the Laws of Lipit-Ištar (§24), dated to the nineteenth century BC, stipulates that the dowry of a man's second wife could only be inherited by that woman's children, not those of the first-ranking wife,[54] thereby potentially effecting the even wider dispersal of goods into the graves of both male and female descendants of the mother. Moreover, according to the Codex Hammurabi (§162), a woman's dowry became the property of her children upon her death and reverted neither to the woman's father who had originally given it nor to her husband.[55] We should note, however, that the payment of brideprice or bridewealth by a man's family to his bride-to-be and her family could have had a similar long-term effect to a dowry—that is, shifting material from one community to another. This will not necessarily be discernible archaeologically, however, particularly in societies where a great deal of wealth may take the form of herds, slaves, or land, all of which are attested as brideprice.[56] Be that as it may, the cases

---

49. Wicks (2019, 195) has suggested that the "combs and multiple mirrors" in tomb JuT1 at Jubaji of Neo-Elamite date may have included "dowry items."

50. Stol 2016, 19; Dalley 1980, 57, 60, 61; Wunsch 2005, 376; Wunsch 2007, 244–45.

51. Wunsch 2005, 371–74.

52. Dalley 1980, 55–56. Compare what Soheila Shahshahani wrote about the Mamasani of western Fars: "Women are at the centre of making a household take its particular identity. This is done by the most basic necessities of a household. . . . The dowry of a woman contains the goods which make a house a Mamassani one" (Shahshahani 2003, 93).

53. Stol 2016, 134.

54. Roth 1995, 31.

55. Roth 1995, 112.

56. Stol 2016, 118.

of Dum Gar Parchinah and Hakalan are particularly ill-suited to a discussion of dowry, or any kind of property transfer, because although twenty prehistoric burials were excavated there, not a single one has been sexed. We can hardly discuss an institution like dowry when we have no idea whether any of the interments at Dum Gar Parchinah and Hakalan were in fact those of females. Moreover, with the possible exception of some inscribed objects, foreign objects acquired originally as bridewealth or dowry are probably impossible to distinguish from those obtained through barter or exchange. Tempting as it might be to talk of dowry in the fifth millennium BC, many obstacles stand in the way of an intelligent assessment.[57]

A FEW WORDS ON THE NOTION OF "TRIBE"

The last topic to be treated here is the tribe as a social construct. As noted above, some scholars have invoked nomadic tribes as the agents of the dispersal of Bakun A culture "over vast areas" and asserted that "we can reasonably demonstrate the presence of nomadic tribes."[58] Nor is such a mechanism limited to Fars, where Tal-e Bakun is located. Rather, in discussing ceramic parallels between sites in the Diyala, the Jabal Hamrin, and the Pusht-e Kuh regions of late fourth and early third millennium BC date, it has been suggested that these were the "result of a coalition and close contact among the mobile pastoral tribes in this region."[59] Let us look at the term *tribe*, particularly in view of the fact that scholars who invoke tribes and draw parallels with modern groups like the Qašqa'i and the Bakhtiyari, rarely if ever define the term.

Although few of my colleagues not concerned with cuneiform law would begin, in the first instance, with the notion of *Hausgemeinschaft*, literally a house and the land appertaining to it, whether communally owned and worked or not, of a single family,[60] in the absence of any evidence to the contrary, this is more or less what most of us probably have in mind when thinking about the smallest unit of social organization in Neolithic and Chalcolithic Iran. Even if the evidence from Tal-e Bakun does not warrant the assumption of social classes, other sites bear witness to significant disparities in wealth. In the fifth millennium BC cemetery at Tol-e Chega Sofla on the Zohreh plain, excavated by Abbas Moghaddam,[61] rich offerings were found in some graves. These included alabaster vessels; seals; copper-bronze weaponry, vessels, disks, and beads; and gold rings, beads, and disks. Cranial modification was also attested, and although we do not know what this means, and whether or not it was a status marker, it was clearly a sign of

57. For bridewealth in the later Sumerian sources see Greengus 1990.
58. Alizadeh 1988, 28.
59. Alizadeh 2010, 371.
60. Koschaker 1933, 72n1.
61. Moghaddam 2016, 2018, 2020.

distinction.[62] Differential access to wealth, as evidenced by smaller and larger multiroomed houses or movable property—we can know nothing of land ownership or herd size—is reasonable to assume given the pronounced variability in mortuary assemblages. But it is important to recognize that all of this evidence pertains to sedentary communities. And thus the question must be asked: where do tribes fit into this discussion?

In his classic study *Nomads of South Persia*, the Norwegian anthropologist Fredrik Barth described the tribe (*il*) as an agglomeration of descent groups or sections (*tira*). These in turn were made up of herding units, usually two to five tents, or families, which banded together and had "freedom of association" on migrations and at campsites comprising ten to forty herding units.[63] In a sense, the tent of the nomad offers a parallel to Weber's *Hausgemeinschaft*. Writing on the origins of the Basseri, Barth noted that, according to their own oral tradition, they had coalesced out of two distinct groups: the Weis, who originated in Khorasan, and the 'Ali Mirzai, who believed they originated locally, in Fars. Yet some sections had different traditions, claiming Qašqa'i and even Arab descent.[64] The fact that tribes are not necessarily composed of genetically related, linguistically homogeneous groups that originated in one area and sprang organically from a kin-related set of people recalls the late Pierre Oberling's definition of Turkic tribes. "Tribe," he wrote, "is a political rather than an ethnic concept. A 'tribe' is a group of families, or clans, whose only bond is their pledge of allegiance to a common chief. . . . Individual tribes tended to be ephemeral," he noted, whereas "the tribal system itself displayed great resilience."[65] Scholars who have invoked the existence of tribes in prehistoric Iran have failed to articulate any details in their conception of what a prehistoric tribe might have looked like, but underlying their discussions is an unstated tenet corresponding to a broad social dichotomy that can be stated succinctly: sedentary communities had one kind of social structure, whatever that may have been, whereas putative nomads were organized as tribes. Given our currently available range of data from later Iranian prehistory, it is difficult, albeit not to say impossible, to see how one might discern those societal features that, for a Barth or an Oberling, characterize tribes in prehistory. Moreover, it is clear, from historical studies of Kurdish tribes, that not all tribes were nomadic; some were sedentary.[66] Whether they had originally been nomadic is beside the point. The question is, can tribal social structure, if by that we mean divisions into descent groups and sections, as well as loyalty to a chief, be maintained in a sedentary

---

62. For the phenomenon more broadly in prehistoric Iran—for example, at Ganj Dareh, Ali Kosh, Tepe Abdul Hosein, Choga Sefid, Choga Mish, and Seh Gabi—see Daems and Croucher (2007); Croucher (2010); and Lorentz (2010).

63. Barth 1961, 22, 25, 38.

64. Barth 1961, 52.

65. Oberling 1964, 98.

66. Sykes 1908, 453, 458–59; Soane 1914, 42, 109, 172, 223, 382.

situation? The answer seems to be most definitely yes. That sedentism and tribalism are not incompatible concepts is well-illustrated elsewhere in the Near East—for example, in Yemen, where, as the late Robert B. Serjeant used to stress, "Tribesmen living in an urban situation could do so for generations without losing their tribal status."[67] Whether the population of Tal-e Bakun A or any other prehistoric community in Iran was organized in a way that might resemble the later tribes of Iran is impossible to say. We have too little data to discern quarters in settlements, a feature often associated with settled tribes living in towns and cities. Moreover, most of the material culture commonly recovered in excavation—mudbrick architecture, ceramics, groundstone, personal ornaments, seals—is simply unsuited to the differentiation of tribal from nontribal social structure. The prudent approach, as I have tried to follow in assessing the likelihood of nomadism in prehistory, is surely not to project a form of social organization onto a prehistoric situation, whether in Iran or anywhere else in the world, for which the evidence simply doesn't exist. Descent groups almost certainly existed in Iran's earliest sedentary communities, but their precise character remains elusive.

---

67. Lewcock 1986, 37.

3

Problems in the Study
of Elamite Kinship

An investigation of Elamite kinship and social structure necessarily relies, first and foremost, on the cuneiform sources found in Iran, which means, principally, those from the site of Susa in Khuzestan (fig. 5). Susa, however, is far from a straightforward case for the simple reason that its population was mixed, containing many Akkadian-speakers;[1] thus, the social institutions attested there may not have been representative of Elam more broadly.

From the fourth millennium BC onward, Susa and other settlements in Khuzestan probably received immigrant settlers from southern Mesopotamia, who, if they did not bring about a political takeover, at least contributed demographically to a more mixed population than would otherwise have been the case. The influence of Mesopotamian customs seems to have been strong in the mid-third millennium BC as well, culminating in the conquest and annexation of Susa and its hinterland by the Akkadians in the twenty-fourth century BC.[2] With the exception of a brief period when Puzur-Inšušinak seized power after the demise of the Akkadian empire,[3] and prior to the city's conquest by Ur-Namma of Ur, c. 2100 BC,[4] Susa was effectively an eastern Mesopotamian city, and it was not until the early second millennium that other dynasties of eastern origin—Šimaški, the *sukkalmah*, and eventually the Middle Elamite kings—stamped their authority on the region and effectively incorporated Susiana and the highlands of Anšan in what is today Fars province and the adjacent mountain valleys into one state. This is what Father Vincent Scheil (fig. 6) presciently referred to in 1901 as the ethnic

---

1. See De Graef (2019, 93–98) on the onomastic and other evidence from Susa of cultural mixing and hybridity.

2. For a convenient summary of the political history of Susa, see Potts 2016, with further literature.

3. Steinkeller 2013.

4. Marchesi 2013.

FIGURE 5. Susa (photo courtesy of the Susa World Heritage Site Archive, ICHTTO, Khuzestan).

dualism of Elam, a topic to which Pierre Amiet[5] and François Vallat returned in the 1970s and 1980s.

Vallat suggested that, because of centuries of Mesopotamian political, cultural, and demographic influence, most of the population of Susiana were Semitic speakers.[6] The late Wilfred G. Lambert wrote of the "Akkadianization of Susiana," just before and after its conquest by the Ur III state.[7] But as Ran Zadok later noted, "quantifiable proof of it exists only in the OB [Old Babylonian] period when the rich documentation provides a sizable prosopographical sample."[8] More recently, the Belgian Assyriologist Katrien De Graef questioned this assessment of Susian society, noting that "only ca. 45% of the personal names" in texts from *sukkalmah*-era Susa "can be identified linguistically and etymologically with certainty as (Sumero-)Akkadian," while a "small part (ca. 15%) can be identified as Elamite and a fairly large part (ca. 40%) is uncertain, hybrid or foreign."[9] Moreover, scholars

5. Scheil 1901, vii; Amiet 1979a, 1979b.
6. Vallat 1980.
7. Lambert 1991.
8. Zadok 2011, 127–28.
9. De Graef 2019, 93.

ND Phot

1665 **2.** *PARIS. — La Sorbonne, Ecole des Hautes Etudes, M. le Professeur Scheil (Assyriologie)*

FIGURE 6. Vincent Scheil (1858–1940) (Bibliothèque Interuniversitaire de la Sorbonne; used with permission under the Creative Commons Attribution Share Alike 3.0 license).

of ancient law and legal institutions have repeatedly emphasized areas in which Susian law differed from that practiced in contemporary Mesopotamia.[10] In what follows, my remarks on Elamite kinship will touch on four areas: filiation, descent, the avunculate, and marriage.

ELAMITE FILIATION

Filiation in ancient Elam has been discussed for almost a century. Both filiation and descent are obviously important, and we may expect them to appear in different contexts. As Katrien De Graef pointed out, Atta-ḫušu is "called 'son of Kindattu' in one text but 'sister's son of Šilhaha' in all other inscriptions."[11] The former is a statement of filiation, the latter, as discussed below, of descent. But if kinship is a cultural construct rather than a diagram of biological filiation, then so, too, are individual designations like father and mother in classificatory systems, as discussed in chapter 1.

A rather naive example of automatically assuming biological filiation wherever the term *father* appears and of completely ignoring the cultural context of its usage is afforded by an analysis of the late twelfth century BC Elamite king,

10. See, e.g., Cuq 1931; Klíma 1963; Korošec 1964; Koschaker 1932, 1933, 1934, 1935a, 1936; Oers 2010, 2013; Badamchi 2018a, 2018b, 2019.

11. De Graef 2012, 541.

Hutelutuš-Inšušinak, and the Elamite royal family, published in 1985.[12] In a brick inscription commemorating the renovation of the temple of "Inšušinak of the grove," Hutelutuš-Inšušinak calls himself "beloved son of Šutruk-Nahhunte, of Kutir-Nahhunte and of Šilhak-Inšušinak," three kings who reigned before him. Is this a recitation of filiation or descent? Was Elamite kinship terminology classificatory or descriptive? In fact, as we know from other inscriptions, Šutruk-Nahhunte was the biological father of Kutir-Nahhunte and his brother Šilhak-Inšušinak, and Šilhak-Inšušinak was the biological father of Hutelutuš-Inšušinak. Hence, in straightforward, descriptive terms, Hutelutuš-Inšušinak's grandfather was Šutruk-Nahhunte, and his paternal uncle was Kutir-Nahhunte. Yet one scholar has written of Hutelutuš-Inšušinak's "triple paternity" because of the fact that he calls himself son of all three of the kings named in the inscription, as if all three were his "father." This has prompted some wild speculation involving Šutruk-Nahhunte's daughter, Nahhunte-Utu, who, it has been suggested, gave birth to Hutelutuš-Inšušinak by her own father in the first alleged case of father-daughter incest in Elamite history; subsequently married Kutir-Nahhunte; and, following his death, her deceased husband's brother, Šilhak-Inšušinak. This scenario, it has been argued, explains the fact that Hutelutuš-Inšušinak refers to himself as the son of three different male forebears. It is more than likely that if a social anthropologist had read Hutelutuš-Inšušinak's brick inscription,[13] he or she would not have leapt to such a convoluted conclusion but would have pointed to the literature on classificatory vs. descriptive kinship systems, discussed in chapter 1, in which numerous males, in addition to Ego's own biological father, may be referred to by a single term translatable as "father."

Whereas descriptive systems retain "specific terms for members of the immediate family, and other terms for more distant, collateral kin," classificatory systems do not "reflect natural degrees of kinship, but lumped together relationships of different kinds under one term." As a result, "the same word might refer, for example, to father, father's brother, father's brother's son, and also perhaps to other relatives, confusing different kinds and degrees of biological relatedness."[14] In both the Crow and Cherokee kinship systems, for example, the sons and grandsons of Ego's father's sister are all called "father." This can result in some of these "fathers" being chronologically younger than Ego. In the Chickasaw system, the son of Ego's father's brother is called father, and this father's sons are called "little father."[15] The organizing principle of the kinship system is the classification of all relatives into one of four clans, those of Ego's mother, Ego's father, Ego's mother's father, and Ego's father's father. "In the father's matrilineal lineage (and clan), for example, all men are 'fathers,'" while "all women of the father's generation and below are

12. Vallat 1985. Cf. Hüsing 1905, 250; and Waters 2000, 26.
13. See, e.g., Vernier 2005. Many more works are cited below.
14. Kuper 1985, 10–11.
15. Eggan 1937, Fig. 1.

'father's sisters,' those above being 'grandmothers' or 'father's sisters,' all husbands of these women are 'grandfathers,' all children are 'father's sisters' and 'fathers.'"[16] An even more extreme example can be found in the well-documented, so-called "Hawaiian" kinship system, which is widespread in Polynesia. In the Hawaiian system, *all* male uncles of Ego, whether on the mother's or the father's side (i.e., mother's brothers and father's brothers), are called "father" or, in Ira Buchler's terms, are "structurally equivalent to the kin type Father."[17] In the Iroquois system, in contrast, the biological father and all of his brothers are referred to as "father" by Ego.

My purpose in mentioning these systems is not to suggest a specific ethnographic parallel to the situation displayed in Hutelutuš-Inšušinak's case, where Ego refers to his biological grandfather, father, and uncle all as "father," but simply to show that there is nothing surprising in the application of one socially constructed term to different biological relatives in Ego's family and no need to assume incest or brother-sister marriage in order to account for the fact that Ego calls multiple individuals "father." Given that the biological relationship of the relatives named by Hutelutuš-Inšušinak is known—Šutruk-Nahhunte was his grandfather, Kutir-Nahhunte was his patrilateral uncle, and Šilhak-Inšušinak was his father—it appears certain that we are dealing with a classic case of classificatory kinship terminology.

One final aspect of filiation on which I wish to comment briefly is the use of the patronymic. This is attested in inscriptions of all sorts. In a well-known text of Šilhak-Inšušinak's reporting on, among other things, his restoration of the temple of Inšušinak at Susa, the Elamite king names all of his predecessors who had restored or renovated the temple. In many cases, the king is identified as PN1, son of PN2.[18] Similarly, on Middle Elamite (late second millennium BC) cylinder seals from Haft Tappeh, one of the most common seal legends is "PN1, son of PN2, servant of PN3 or Deity 1."[19] Even briefer legends of the form PN1, son of PN2, such as "Huban-kitin son of Šutur-Nahhunte" or "Kitepatin son of Pinririra," appear on later Neo-Elamite seals.[20] In the late Neo-Elamite era (mid-first millennium BC), as the inscribed objects from Kalmākarra cave clearly show, this sort of identification was the norm. There we find the formula PN1 + Patronymic (son of PN2) repeated many times, for example *Hamfriš son of *Tapala-; Unzi-kilik, son of *Hamfriš; Ahtir, son of *Hamfriš; Untaš, son of Huban; and so forth. In these cases, filiation is stated, presumably, for purposes of identification—to make it easier to distinguish homonymous individuals bearing the same name, in this case *Hamfriš—and would seem to satisfy a strictly utilitarian requirement. But apart

---

16. Eggan 1937, 45.
17. Buchler 1964, 291.
18. König 1965, 110.
19. Mofidi-Nasrabadi 2011, 296–298. PN = personal name.
20. Amiet 1973, 30, no. 40; Vallat 2002.

from the fact that the use of patronymics was obviously helpful in cases where more than one individual had the same name,[21] the use of the patronymic may also have been a marker of social status. In this case, the phrase "son of PN2" functions like a title. Certainly, all of the individuals whose names appear on the Kalmākarra objects were of high status. This is implied by the fact that all of the objects on which their names were inscribed were made of either gold or silver. But the name Unsak is also attested in Neo-Elamite texts from the Acropole at Susa, without a patronymic,[22] and one wonders if this was not just because the name appeared in a short economic text, where there was no need (or room) for specificity, but because the socioeconomic status of the individual named was low.

ELAMITE DESCENT AND ASCRIBED
GROUP AFFILIATION

Three issues concerned with the broader topic of descent have attracted attention in scholarship on the Elamite sources: descent and ascribed group affiliation; descent and succession; and the avunculate.

The topic of descent and ascribed group affiliation was raised in 1907 by Vincent Scheil in a discussion of the use of the gentilic *Unsakpera* in some Acropole texts from Susa. Scheil interpreted this term as "someone of the *gens* of Unsak" or, more simply stated, "the Unsakian."[23] But since Unsak is a personal name rather than a toponym, the term *Unsakians* did not denote the residents of a geographical locale but rather "the people" of Unsak, in the sense of his descendants. This illustrates what Rüdiger Schmitt termed the *Propatronymikon*—an ancestral name derived from that of an eponymous ancestor that indicated tribal or lineage membership rather than filiation.[24] In 2002, François Vallat suggested that *Unsakpera*, while derived from a personal rather than a geographical name, designated members of a nomadic tribe, the eponymous founder of which bore the name Unsak.[25] We have no way of verifying the truth of this assertion, but it is clear that comparable tribal designations current among the Chaldaean and Aramaean tribes of southern and southeastern Babylonia in the first millennium BC did not apply exclusively to nomadic groups.[26] Similarly, contemporary urban Babylonian kingroups organized by descent from an eponymous ancestor and called names like

---

21. Henkelman 2003, table 2.

22. Scheil 1907, 62, no. 68, line 11; 68, no. 79, line 4; and 128, no. 143, line 2.

23. Scheil 1907, 9.

24. Schmitt (2002, 364) wrote: "(wenn statt der Vatersangabe die Abstammung von einem früheren Ahnen bezeichnet wird). Alternative Namenzusätze sind die Angabe der Sippenzugehörigkeit (mittels Pluralgenetiv der Sippenbezeichnung) oder die der lokalen Herkunft (etwa des Wohn- oder Geburtsortes)."

25. Vallat 2002.

26. Brinkman 1968.

Šumu-lubši and Egibi, after "the personal name of the lineage's supposed ancestor," were certainly not nomads.[27]

DESCENT AND SUCCESSION

A striking manifestation of descent as a justification for the right of succession is found in the "Berlin Letter." Published in 1986 by the late Jan van Dijk,[28] this literary text from Babylon, of Neo-Babylonian date, purports to be a letter to the Kassite court from an Elamite king who was married to a daughter of the Kassite king Meli-šipak (1180–72 BC). In it, the Elamite complains bitterly that, by virtue of his descent, he should be seated on the Kassite throne. In the text, not all of which is preserved, the writer, whom we may call Ego, enumerates at least four generations of ancestors who had married Kassite princesses, identified not by name but as "daughter of Kassite King X," one of whom was a daughter of "the mighty King Kurigalzu." Thus, matrilineal descent from a long line of Kassite princesses and, by extension, kings, coupled with patrilineal descent from four generations or more of Elamite kings belonging to what has *ex post facto* been termed the "Igihalkid" dynasty, after the presumed founder of the dynasty, Igi-halki, were invoked by Ego to justify his claim to the Babylonian throne. "Why I, who am a king, son of a king, seed of a king, scion of a king, who am king (?) for the lands, the land of Babylonia and for the land of Elam, descendant of the eldest daughter of mighty King Kurigalzu, (why) do I not sit on the throne of the land of Babylonia?" he complains. "I sent you a sincere proposal, you however have granted me no reply; you may climb up to heaven [but I'll pull you down] by your hem, you may go down to hell, [but I'll pull you up] by your hair! I shall destroy your cities, demolish your fortresses, stop up your (irrigation) ditches, cut down your orchards, [pull out] the rings (of the sluices) at the mouths of your (irrigation) canals," he threatens.

Because of their well-known campaigns against Babylonia, either Šutruk-Nahhunte or his son Kutir-Nahhunte have previously been considered the most likely author of this letter. Recently, however, Susanne Paulus has suggested that the writer was Kidin-Hutran II, whose Babylonian campaign in 1224 BC, recounted in a text known as Chronicle P, resulted in the overthrow of Enlil-nadin-šumi, an Assyrian puppet who had been installed by the Assyrian king Tukulti-Ninurta I following his defeat of Kaštiliašu I about a year earlier. This illegitimate king's occupation of the Babylonian throne, Paulus suggested, was the trigger for Kidin-Hutran's rage at having his rightful succession usurped by someone with no just claim to kingship.[29] In 2017, Michael Roaf reassessed all of the data in the Berlin Letter,

27. Nielsen 2011, 1–2, with extensive bibliography.

28. Van Dijk 1986. The principal later studies on the letter are Goldberg 2004; Quintana 2010; Paulus 2013; Potts 2016; and Roaf 2017.

29. For previous scholarship see van Dijk 1986.

including alternate suggestions by Jeremy Goldberg.[30] Roaf concluded that contradictions between Kassite and Elamite chronology and succession, as recounted on the Šilhak-Inšušinak stele, were irreconcilable but could be attributed to the fact that the Berlin Letter is a literary rather than historical work. For my purposes, however, it is still significant, for the Berlin Letter offers a perfect example of what the American anthropologist G. P. Murdock termed "double descent"—that is, "a combination of matrilineal and patrilineal descent, the two modes of affiliation being followed concurrently." In such cases. Murdock continued, "there are necessarily at least two coexistent and intersecting sets of kin-groups—lineages, sibs, or moieties—the one matrilineal and the other patrilineal."[31] Moreover, the data presented in the Berlin Letter is precisely the opposite of the "genealogical amnesia," to borrow Clifford Geertz's phrase,[32] that is often deployed to fabricate or falsify alliances and descent groups.[33] Rather, notwithstanding its literary character and Roaf's comments, the text deploys descent in an unambiguous fashion to justify the writer's claim to rightful succession.

THE AVUNCULATE

The third aspect of descent to be discussed here is the avunculate, a topic that has loomed large in the study of Elam since the late nineteenth century. The Dutch scholar Jan N. Bremmer referred to the avunculate as the "more cordial, affectionate relationship between the mother's brother . . . and the sister's son."[34] The convoluted history of its treatment in Elamite studies began even before the first discovery of cuneiform tablets at Susa. In 1884, Theophilus G. Pinches, the great British Museum cuneiformist of the late nineteenth and early twentieth centuries, published a discussion of a text known as Babylonian Chronicle 1. There we read, "In the fifth year of Merodach-Baladan [II, i.e., 717 BC], Ummanigaš [Huban-nikaš I], king of Elam, died, and was succeeded by Ištar-hundu [Šutruk-Nahhunte II], *his sister's son*."[35]

More evidence of relevance appeared when Scheil published several texts from Susa, in one of which the late second millennium BC, Middle Elamite ruler Humban-numena was identified as sister's son of Šilhaha (EKI 39m). The extant Elamite royal inscriptions, most particularly a large, fragmentary stele of Šilhak-Inšušinak's (c. 1155–25 BC) excavated at Susa in 1902 and known as EKI 48, identify

30. Goldberg 2004.

31. Murdock 1940, 555, 557.

32. See Geertz 1964.

33. As Digard (1987, 18) noted, "genealogical amnesia" is a device deployed in the ex post facto fabrication of alliances, affiliations, and political regroupings justified in terms of descent.

34. Bremmer 1976, 65.

35. Pinches 1884, 199. Full references for what follows are found in Potts 2018a.

no fewer than eleven rulers in the *sukkalmah* period (early second millennium BC) as "sister's son of PN":[36]

1. Idaddu I, sister's son of Ḫutran-Tepti (EKI 48)
2. Attaḫušu, sister's son of Šilḫaḫa (EKI 48; UAA 191)
3. Kuk-Kirwaš, sister's son of Šilḫaḫa (EKI 38)
4. Širukduḫ I, sister's son of Šilḫaḫa (EKI 48)
5. Ṣiwepalarḫuḫpak, sister's son of Širukduh (EKI 3 and 48)
6. Kuduzuluš, sister's son of Širukduh (UAA 195)
7. Temti-Agun, sister's son of Širukduh (UAA 196)
8. Kuk-Našur II, sister's son of Temti-Agun, sister's son of Šilḫaḫa (UAA 198; EKI 38a)
9. Širukduḫ II, sister's son of Kuk-Našur II (UAA 199)
10. Temti-ḫalki, sister's son of Šilḫaḫa (EKI 48; UAA 200)
11. Kuk-Našur IV, sister's son of Tan-Uli (EKI 48)

In the later second millennium BC, during the Middle Elamite period, only Ḫumban-numena was identified as sister's son of Šilḫaḫa (EKI 39m), while in the early first millennium BC, during the Neo-Elamite period, as shown by Pinches, only Šutruk-Naḫḫunte II was called sister's son of Huban-Nikaš I.[37]

The sister's son has been a figure of special significance all over the world, from antiquity to the modern day. Had Pinches or Scheil looked into the extensive literature on this topic already available in their lifetimes, they would have found ample evidence of this phenomenon and simply added Elam to the long list of cultures in which the sister's son enjoyed preferential status. Unfortunately, this was not the case. Rather, the course of the discussion of this topic was completely distorted in 1926 by F. W. König, who alleged that the sister's son in Elam was the male offspring of a sibling marriage between the Elamite ruler and his biological sister.[38] The fundamental logic or illogic followed by many of the scholars who have written on this topic may be reduced to three simple propositions: first, Elamite royal inscriptions identify more than a dozen kings (noted above) who are identified by the epithet "sister's son of X"; second, as "normal" royal succession "always" passes from father to son, the sister's son must have been a son born of a king's own sister—that is, a product of incestuous sibling marriage; and third, the stipulated filiation from a female, identified as the presumed previous ruler's sister, implies matrilineal succession.

---

36. Taken from Soldt 1990, 587.

37. Grayson 1975, 75; Pinches 1884, 199.

38. König 1926a. Cf. König 1964. See also Vallat 1996, 300: "fils que le roi NP a eu avec sa propre sœur." Cf. Frandsen 2009, 123: "the son whom the king had with his own sister." Waters (2006, 502) even invoked incest as the root cause of the health problems (stroke, mysterious death) suffered by several Neo-Elamite kings who were brothers—that is, Huban-ḫaltas II, Urtak, and Teʾumman. Gorris (2014, 74) showed, however, "that Huban-haltash II died of a natural cause and that Urtak & Tepti-Huban-Inshushinak I [Teʾumman] were most likely murdered."

FIGURE 7. Hanni and his family in the rock relief of Eškaft-e Salman II (photo: courtesy of Javier Álvarez-Mon).

Fundamentally, as the comparative study of political institutions around the world quickly demonstrates, the assumption that succession *naturally* passes from father to son is a completely ethnocentric notion. This flawed assumption, exacerbated by a complete indifference to and ignorance of the large body of literature on the historical importance of the sister's son, spawned the theory of incestuous, brother-sister marriage between Elamite rulers and their sisters. Yet, although François Vallat could not conceive of an Elamite monarch willingly ceding succession to his sororal nephew rather than his biological son,[39] and Walther Hinz considered "Geschwisterehe" a defining characteristic of the Elamite state,[40] these views are completely unsupported by the evidence. There is nothing in the phrase "sister's son" that justifies an assumption of incest; in fact, before the

39. Thus, to paraphrase Vallat (1996, 300), it would seem at the very least curious for a rich and powerful man to favor his nephews at the expense of his children, above all in the Orient, where, to this day, the son embodies not only a form of insurance in old age for the parents but the guarantor of their well-being in the hereafter.

40. According to Hinz (1964, 76), brother-sister marriage, levirate (see below), and a tripartite division of authority defined Elam. Nothing like it ever existed on Earth, he believed. Wider reading would have disabused Hinz of the mistaken belief that such institutions had never existed anywhere on Earth but in Elam.

Achaemenid period, there is no undisputed evidence of any royal incest in Elam. The only possible exception to this statement occurs in a Neo-Elamite inscription accompanying the rock relief of the local ruler (*kutur*) Ḫanni of Ayapir, son of Tahhi, at Šekaft-e Salman IIIB, near Malamir (fig. 7).[41] The text refers to *Ḫuḫin rutu šutu ḫanik urina*, which scholars have translated variously as "Ḫuḫin, his wife-and-sister,"[42] "my beloved sister-wife,"[43] and "my beloved spouse-sister."[44] The Spanish Elamologist Enrique Quintana has suggested, however, that the expression *rutu šutu* should not be understood as "spouse-sister" but rather as lawful or true wife.[45]

In fact, if, as suggested above, the Elamite kinship system was classificatory rather than descriptive, then the term *sister* may denote a potentially large array of female relatives. Yet even a more literal understanding of the term need not imply that Ego was the son of an incestuous union between a king and his biological sister. Innumerable cases scattered widely in both time and space attest to the preferential position enjoyed by the king's sister's son, both in royal succession and in nonroyal cases of inheritance, around the world. Out of the abundant literary, historical, and anthropological attestations of the sister's son may be selected just a few examples.

To begin with the extant body of Western literary evidence, Cú Chulainn, Beowulf, Tristan and Parzival, to name just a few literary figures, are all identified as "sister's sons" in the epics in which they appear. Critical studies by F. J. Gummere,[46] W. O. Farnsworth,[47] C. H. Bell,[48] T. J. Garbáty,[49] R. H. Bremmer,[50] and T. Ó Cathasaigh[51] clearly demonstrate both how common and how important this social category was in medieval Europe. Moving from the realm of literature to history, we find many examples of sister's sons enjoying special status. In the kingdom of Ellipi, just to the north of Elam in what is today Luristan, two brothers, Nibê and Ašpabara, who were the sons of the sister of king Daltâ, disputed the succession to the throne upon Dalta's death in 708/7 BC.[52] By contrast, Daltâ's own son, Lutû, was not considered a candidate for the succession. Roughly a thousand years later

41. EKI 76. For the relief and earlier bibliography, see Waters 2000, 82–85; and Álvarez-Mon 2019, 38, 44–46.

42. Stolper 1987–90, 278.

43. Glassner 1994, 222. Cf. Grillot 1988, 53n21: Huhin, spouse-sister, my beloved.

44. Cf. Hinz 1962, 112.

45. Quintana 2010, 52n40: "my beloved true wife." Cf. König 1965, 161: Huhin, my chosen/beloved lawful spouse. Soldt (1990, 588) queried whether Hanni was in fact married to his sister.

46. Gummere 1901.

47. Farnsworth 1913.

48. Bell 1922.

49. Garbáty 1977.

50. Bremmer 1980.

51. Ó Cathasaigh 1986.

52. Fuchs 2003, 130.

Charlemagne's sister's son Roland appears;[53] and in the early eighth century, the Orkhon inscriptions honoring Kül Tegin and his brother Bilgä Kagan were erected by Yolig Tegin, their sister's son.[54] Among the Picts, succession to kingship ran through the sister's son.[55] Tancred, who took command of the First Crusade after the capture of Bohemund of Antioch in the early twelfth century, was Bohemund's sister's son.[56] In India, the fifteenth-century Italian traveler Ludovico di Varthema found that "the kings of Calicut appointed the sister's son as heir to the throne, being sure that they two were of the same blood,"[57] and, in fact, the uncertain paternity of a king's son—that is, the suspicion that the queen or king's consort had been impregnated by someone other than the king—is often invoked as an evolutionary argument in favor of the preferential position of the sister's son for, even if a king could not be certain that he was the real father of a male child born of his wife, the king always knew with certainty that the child of his sister was of his own blood.[58]

Among the vast number of ethnographic examples illustrating the importance of the sister's son that could be cited, just a few will be noted here. In 1811, the French Orientalist Étienne-Marc Quatremère observed that, among the Bedja, who lived in parts of what is today Eritrea, Sudan, and the eastern desert of Egypt, succession passed from a chief to his sister's son, and he went on to compare this custom with what he had read in an unpublished manuscript entitled a "Relation of What Passed in New-France, on the Great St. Lawrence River, In 1634," by the Jesuit missionary Paul Le Jeune (1591–1664), who had observed the same practice among the Algonquin and Huron.[59] In 1877 the renowned nineteenth-century American scholar Lewis Henry Morgan said of an Ojibwa chief who died around 1840: "His son could not succeed him. . . . The right of succession belonged to his nephew, E-kwä'-ka-mik, who must have the office. This nephew was a son of one of his sisters."[60] Similarly, in the Delaware tribe, the son of a deceased chief was disallowed from succeeding his father because "he was of another gens"—that is, a consanguineous group descended from a common ancestor, distinguished by name and bound by blood ties—as a result of which the chief "was succeeded by his nephew . . . a son of one of the sisters of the deceased" chief, who was considered to belong to the same gens.[61] And similarly, in Fiji, as Lorimer Fison wrote to Morgan in 1879, "My father's sister is my mother and calls me her son, my mother's

---

53. Farnsworth 1913, 199–200.
54. Ross 1930, 864.
55. Zimmer 1894, 218. Cf. Kornemann 1925, 357.
56. Tritton and Gibb 1933, 72, 74.
57. Cited in Farnsworth 1913, 232; and Garbáty 1977, 224.
58. Fortunato 2012, 4940.
59. Quatremère 1811, 136n1.
60. Morgan 1877, 170–71n3.
61. Morgan 1877, 63.

brother is my father, and calls me his son. And in that tribe the chief's sister's son succeeds to the exclusion of the chief's own son."[62] Moreover, among the Trobriand islanders, "The chief was succeeded by his sister's son. His own son had no place in the new dispensation—unless he was married into the new chief's family. Therefore as an infant he was betrothed to his father's sister's daughter, making him the brother-in-law of the next chief."[63] The same was true throughout Melanesia, where R. H. Codrington found that "succession to property of all kinds is regularly and properly with the sister's son."[64] While these examples could be multiplied many times over, they suffice to demonstrate that, far from being an aberration occasioned by royal sibling marriage, succession to high office and inheritance by the sister's son is a phenomenon attested in societies all over the world and in many different periods. Just one final historical example should be mentioned though, which, had more scholars paid attention to it, could have pointed the way toward an understanding of the avunculate in Elam well over a century ago.

In his *Germania* (20.4), the Roman historian Tacitus (c. 56–120 AD) wrote, "Sister's children [*Sororum filiis*] mean as much to their uncle [*avunculus*] as to their father, some tribes regard this blood-tie as even closer and more sacred than that between son and father, and in taking hostages make it the basis of their demand, as though they thus secure loyalty more surely and have a wider hold on the family." In 1748 Montesquieu famously commented on this passage in book 18 of his *De l'esprit des lois*. There he wrote that Tacitus's remark explained the particular love that early Frankish kings had for their sisters and the children of their sisters, such as Gunthram and his nephew Childebert,[65] who, according to Gregory of Tours, were regarded as the king's own children and the king's wife as their own mother.[66] A few years later, in 1755, the French historian Jean-Philippe-René de La Blèterie (1696–1772) published a translation and commentary on Tacitus in which he asked, why, in certain Germanic city-states, a father gave preference to his sister's son rather than his own children. Was it because paternity is often "equivocal," as he put it? He went on to express no surprise that this should be the case in Asia and Africa. But, in light of what Tacitus wrote about the sanctity of marriage among the Germans, he was surprised to find preferential succession by the sister's son there, although he decided that perhaps not all Germanic societies were as moral as the most noble ones described by Tacitus.[67]

In 1887, when the German ancient historian Hugo Winckler published his own edition, together with J. N. Strassmaier, of Pinches's Babylonian Chronicle 1, naming Šutruk-Nahhunte II as his uncle Huban-nikaš I's successor, he immediately

---

62. Stern 1930, 272–73.
63. Kuper 2008, 726.
64. Codrington 1889, 312.
65. Brehaut 1916, 212–13, bk. 9.20.
66. Montesquieu 1845, 243.
67. La Blèterie 1755, 162–64.

thought of the Tacitus passage on the sister's son, although he did not say this at the time. Fourteen years later, in 1901, however, in his review of Scheil's first volume of Akkadian texts from Susa,[68] which included inscribed bricks of Kuk-Kirwaš, Temti-ḫalki, and Attaḫušu in which the phrase "sister's son of Šilḫaḫa" appeared, Winckler drew his readers' attention to the Tacitean passage on the sister's son. There, Winckler noted that he had first thought of the association between the Elamite sister's son and the passage in Tacitus when he edited the Babylonian Chronicle with Strassmaier in 1887.[69] The new texts from Susa, Winckler suggested, showed that the passage in the Chronicle was not an aberration and justified drawing a parallel with Tacitus. Had Winckler's insight been followed, we should have been spared more than a century of scholarship invoking brother-sister incestuous marriage in the misinterpretation of the sister's son in Elam. Yet, as we have seen, F. W. König's salacious perspective captured more attention than Winckler's judicious approach.

There remain two outstanding questions, however, that must be addressed. The first concerns the use of the epithet "sister's son" by rulers who lived long after their named uncle. It is entirely possible that Attahušu, the first Elamite to identify himself as Šilhaha's sister's son, may actually have been Šilhaha's biological nephew. But the Middle Elamite ruler Ḫumban-numena, who also called himself "sister's son of Šilhaha," lived centuries later and was separated from Šilhaha by the reigns of at least eight kings. How can this be explained? Perhaps an insight from medieval Germanic epic will be useful.

In 1922, Clair Hayden Bell noted that the terms for maternal uncle and nephew, ôheim and neve, were sometimes applied "as complimentary titles of people who bear no blood relationship to the speaker, and even more frequently . . . in the sense of a distant relative in general."[70] But in addition to establishing descent, such an association may be a device to enhance the epic stature of Ego, as in Beowulf, whose titular hero boasts of his famous kinsmen.[71] Similarly, an observation by the American anthropologist G. P. Murdock is potentially enlightening with respect to the "sister's son" in Elam. Commenting on the matrilineages of the Bantu-speaking Venda, documented by the British anthropologist H. A. Stayt, Murdock noted that these "are linked primarily with the ancestor cult."[72] A reference to "sister's son of Šilhaha" by a king who lived seven hundred years later than Šilhaha may have served a similar function—that is, to ally Ego with the charisma and heroic qualities of an ancestor, whether biologically related or not, in order to confer a benefit

68. Scheil 1900.
69. Winckler 1901a, 449.
70. Bell 1922, 78.
71. Garbáty 1977, 228.
72. Murdock 1940, 555–58.

on Ego, "a quasi-evolutionary, selective advantage out of all proportion to biological reality."[73]

The second question concerns the relationship of the epithet "sister's son," succession, and matrilinearity. This idea originated in Winckler's review of Scheil's first volume of Akkadian texts from Susa mentioned above. There, Winckler suggested that the status of the sister's son in Elamite royal succession was a marker of matriarchy and residual polygamy.[74] Four years later Georg Hüsing described Elamite succession as matrilineal,[75] and in his influential, if flawed, 1926 article on matrilinearity and succession in ancient Elam F. W. König interpreted *ruhu šak* as an epithet for male descendants of the female founder of the Elamite dynastic line.[76] In fact, "Elamite Matriarchy" formed an entire chapter in Ernst Herzfeld's posthumously published collection of studies that appeared in 1968 as *The Persian Empire*. Among the topics covered there were "Matrilinear Succession in Elam," "Matriarchal Family Excludes Brother-Sister-Marriage," and "'Adoption' in Matrilinear Succession."[77] Although he was critical of both König and Koschaker, the Soviet Azeri Orientalist Yusuf B. Yusifov maintained, in 1974, that in the early second millennium BC, the "matrilineal principle of succession" had prevailed, whereas in the Middle Elamite period, it was superseded by "the patrilineal principle of succession."[78] And as recently as 2018, Behzad Mofidi-Nasrabadi suggested that the prominence of figures whom he interpreted as royal Elamite women on early second-millennium BC cylinder seals "probably arises from the significant social role of women in the Elamite community and could go back to a matrilineal form of social organization often proposed for the early era of Elamite history."[79] None of the Elamite evidence, however, demonstrates that Elam, in any period, was a matriarchal society or observed strict matrilineal succession. Moreover, an abundance of anthropological and literary evidence shows that the avunculate and matrilinearity are not necessarily linked. Robert Lowie, for example, found "the avunculate among patrilineal Melanesians, such as Torres Strait Islanders,"[80] and H. A. Stayt noted that among the Bantu-speaking Venda, where the matrilineage exerted "a stronger emotional and personal influence" on individuals than the patrilineage did, "descent, succession, and inheritance" were *all* reckoned through the father's side.[81] Similarly, in the twelfth-century romance *Perceval le Gallois*, by Chrétien de Troyes, the male protagonists are "physically and politically supreme

73. Potts 2018a, 544.

74. Winckler 1901a, 449.

75. Hüsing 1905, 250.

76. König 1926a, 536.

77. Herzfeld 1968, 259–74.

78. Yusifov 1974, 331. For a different perspective, see Quintana 2016.

79. Mofidi-Nasrabadi 2018, 245.

80. Lowie 1918, 532. This point was also echoed by Oswald Szemerényi, albeit in the context of Indo-European kinship terminology. See Szemerényi 1977, 184.

81. Stayt 1931, 185.

. . . yet filiation" was reckoned "on the side of the woman."[82] We should also note, as R. S. P. Beekes did in 1976, that the important passage in Tacitus's *Germania*, discussed above, while stressing the importance of the sister's son, went on to say that "a man's own children are his heirs and successors, and there is no power of bequest."[83]

THE LEVIRATE

The final topic to be addressed here is levirate marriage, not because it is something for which we have good evidence but simply because it has been identified since the early twentieth century as a characteristic of ancient Elam. In 1905 Scheil published a short dedication to the deity Manzat, inscribed on a stone door socket, in which the Elamite king Hutelutuš-Inšušinak identified himself as son of Kutir-Nahhunte and Šilhak-Inšušinak.[84] When he published a full edition of the text in 1911, Scheil suggested that Hutelutuš-Inšušinak had identified one biological and one adoptive father, adoptive in the sense that if Kutir-Nahhunte and Nahhunte-Utu were his biological parents, then following the death of his father, Kutir-Nahhunte, Šilhak-Inšušinak became Hutelutuš-Inšušinak's adoptive parent by marrying the latter's mother.[85] König believed, however, that from a juridical perspective, the marriage of a widow by the deceased's younger brother was a form of adoption.[86]

In 1933 the great Austrian comparative legal scholar Paul Koschaker became the first scholar to classify Šilhak-Inšušinak's marriage with his brother's widow as a case of levirate.[87] The *locus classicus* of the so-called law of levirate is Deuteronomy 25:5–6, which enjoins one brother, in the event of the death of another who is married but childless, to "go in unto her, and take her to him to wife, and perform the duty of an husband's brother unto her. And it shall be, that the firstborn which she beareth shall succeed in the name of his brother which is dead, that his name be not put out of Israel."[88] It is important to recognize, however, that the biblical law of levirate has a close parallel in the Middle Assyrian laws (§30), where we read that in the event of the death of a married son, "the father who presented the bridal gift [brideprice]"—that is, the widow's father-in-law—if he "so pleases, he shall take

82. Nitze 1912, 299.

83. Beekes 1976, 45.

84. Scheil 1905 = EKI 65. Cf. the discussion at the beginning of this chapter.

85 Scheil 1911, 70.

86. König 1964, 226. Cf. Burrows 1940, 5. Michaelis (1786, 184) maintained, however, that levirate was not a form of adoption. For a cross-cultural study of adoption see Goody 1969.

87. Koschaker 1933, 59. Cf. Koschaker 1935a, 72–73.

88. I quote here from the King James Version. For just a few of the many discussions of this text published over the years, see Zschokke 1883, 125–26; Mielziner 1901, 54–58; Greenspahn 1994, 52–54; and Volgger 2002.

his daughter-in-law . . . and give her in marriage to his (second) son."[89] A similar provision, though with extenuating ramifications,[90] appears in the Hittite laws, where we read (§193), "If a man has a wife, and the man dies, his brother shall take his widow as wife. (If the brother dies,) his father shall take her. When afterwards his father dies, his (i.e., the father's) brother shall take the woman whom he had."[91]

The biblical evidence of levirate has been discussed for centuries. To cite just a few of the many studies that are relevant to this subject, in the twelfth century, the Sephardic philosopher Moses Maimonides (1138–1204) examined levirate in his commentary on the Mishneh.[92] In 1639, the law of levirate was discussed by Johannes Buxtorf (1564–1629) in his *Lexicon Chaldaicum Talmudicum et Rabinicum*,[93] and in 2009 Devora Weisberg published a book on the levirate in ancient Judaism. In 1915 and 1916, respectively, the Indo-Iranian philologist and rabbi Isidor Scheftelowitz and the American linguistic anthropologist Edward Sapir both wrote at some length on the levirate. Scheftelowitz, on the one hand, believed that the law of levirate in ancient Israel arose on "agro-political grounds" to prevent the diminution of a family's landholdings by a widow's exogamous marriage that resulted in her property passing to another family.[94] Sapir, on the other hand, examined the institution and associated kinship vocabulary among the Upper Chinook of Washington State and the Yahi or Southern Yana of Northern California. He cited cases where the terms for paternal uncle and stepfather are identical, as are the terms for a man's brother's son and a man's stepson, or a man's brother's daughter and a man's stepdaughter. In fact, as Sapir reported, his Yahi informant "made it perfectly clear that he himself looked upon the facts"—that is, the kinship terms—"as simply another way of saying that it was customary for the widow to marry her former husband's brother and for the widower to marry his former wife's sister."[95] In contrast to Scheftelowitz, Max Weber argued that the levirate was a response to the very real threat of the extinction of a tribe through the death of its warriors and an attempt to ensure that a family was not left defenseless

---

89. Puukko 1949; Roth 1995, 164; Lafont 1999, 152n74.

90. Thus, Tylor (1889, 253) argued that "the word 'levirate,' from *levir* = husband's brother, has become the accepted term for this institution, but its sense must in most cases be extended to take in a series of kinsmen, among whom the brother-in-law only ranks first."

91. Hoffner, in Roth 1995, 236. Cf. Lafont 1999, 176–77 and note 20.

92. Pocock 1655, 55; Lewis 1725, 269–72; Fürstenthal 1842, 32. Note Rowley (1947, 77), who stressed that "while the later scholasticism of the Talmud may preserve some ancient traditions, it cannot be implicitly trusted to throw light on customs which were already obsolete when the book of Ruth was written, needing to be explained to the reader as customs that formerly held in Israel."

93. Buxtorf 1639, 928, "Leviratio, Affinitas talis."

94. Scheftelowitz 1915, 255. Cf. Westbrook 1991, 76–77: "We are of the opinion that all three biblical sources reflect an institution with a single legal object: to prevent extinction of the deceased's title to his landed inheritance."

95. Sapir 1916, 329–30.

in the event of a husband or father's demise.[96] In contrast, Yusifov believed that Šilhak-Inšušinak married his brother's widow "in order to weaken . . . possible claims to the throne," presumably from a rival who interposed himself in the line of succession such that "this marriage . . . was caused by . . . necessity, not by the formal observation of the custom of levirate."[97]

To his credit, Scheftelowitz cited a wide range of ethnographic parallels to illustrate the widespread, if not necessarily uniform, application of the law of levirate.[98] It is unnecessary to delve too deeply into this material, but perhaps one example from the Mota of Melanesia will show just why the custom, whether in its purest form or in a variant involving a kinsman other than a younger brother of the deceased, is so common. Among the Mota, as R. H. Codrington noted,

> the Levirate obtains as a matter of course, so far as that a woman who has become the widow of one member of a family connexion remains as the wife of another member of the same. A wife is obtained by a certain payment, towards which the near relations of the bridegroom, both on the father's and mother's side, contribute; it is arranged, therefore, in case of death to which the member of the family connexion it will be most convenient and economical that the widow should pass, whether brother, uncle, or cousin of the deceased, of course of his own kin.[99]

And as Leslie White emphasized, "families became units in the cooperative process as well as individuals. Marriages came to be contracts between families, later between even larger groups. The individual lost much of his initiative in courtship and choice of mates, for it was now a group affair." Thus, with both levirate and its counterpart sororate, in which a deceased female's sister marries her former brother-in-law, White observed, "the group character of marriage is manifest. Each group of consanguinei supplies a member of the other group with a spouse. If the spouse dies, the relatives of the deceased must supply another to take his or her place. The alliance between families is important and must be continued; even death cannot part them."[100]

The discussion of the levirate in Elam was prompted in large part by EKI 60 and 65, in which Hutelutuš-Inšušinak identified himself as son of Kutir-Nahhunte and Šilhak-Inšušinak. The evidence I have reviewed here shows that there is nothing inherently implausible about the existence of the law of levirate in Elam, given its attestation in the Hittite, Middle Assyrian, and Deuteronomic laws. Two points, however, raise doubts about the use of Hutelutuš-Inšušinak's stated filiation as evidence of levirate in Elam. The first is the absence of evidence in earlier legal texts

96. See Hellmann and Palyi 1923, 47–48.

97. Yusifov 1974, 326.

98. Tylor (1889, 253) noted that "the levirate appears in its various forms among one hundred and twenty peoples in my list, or about one in three in the world."

99. Codrington 1889, 308. Similarly, there are numerous variants of levirate in Africa that go beyond the original biblical legal definition. See the papers in Radcliffe-Brown and Forde 1950.

100. White 1948, 425.

from Susa[101] of any reference to levirate marriage there. The second, more fundamental concern, arises from those texts in which Hutelutuš-Inšušinak is identified as son of Šutruk-Nahhunte (his biological grandfather), Kutir-Nahhunte (his
paternal uncle), and Šilhak-Inšušinak (his biological father), not just of his putative biological (*pater*) and *levir* fathers. In view of everything said above about classificatory vs. descriptive kinship terms, we should be very wary of interpreting the
statement that Hutelutuš-Inšušinak was literally or biologically the "son" of these
"fathers," thereby automatically imputing the institution of levirate to the Elamites.
Until additional evidence becomes available, it would be prudent to reserve judg-
ment on the existence of the levirate in ancient Elam, particularly at Susa.

---

101 See Sadafi 2013; and Badamchi 2018a.

4

Descent and Marriage
in Achaemenid Iran

With the Medes and Persians we leave the realm of what are often considered the aboriginal peoples of the Iranian plateau and lowland Khuzestan and enter the Indo-European or Indo-Iranian realm. The evidence from the earlier and mid-first millennium BC raises a number of important questions, only a few of which will be considered here.

MEDES, ACHAEMENIDS, AND THE TRIBAL QUESTION

The ancient historian Albert Ten Eyck Olmstead considered the Medes "essentially nomadic, though they had been settled long enough in the mountains to have taken on some of the characteristics of a sedentary people."[1] Nevertheless, the Neo-Assyrian sources make it clear that the Median landscape was dominated by towns, villages, and fortresses overseen by *bēl āli* (city lords).[2] Discussing "the Median people"—for which he uses the Greek noun *ethnos* (ἔθνος)—Herodotus (*Hist.* 1.101) lists the names of six Median genea (γένεα), tribes or descent groups: the Busae, Paretaceni, Struchates, Arizanti, Budii, and Magi. In analyzing Herodotus's use of the terms *ethnos* and *genos*, Christopher P. Jones noted that "while he might mean the second to be a subdivision of the first"—that is, the *genea* (tribes or descent groups) to be subsets of the Median *ethnos* (people or nation)—"he could equally well be referring to these six groups as hereditary" or, as he put it, "united by birth," or "a genetic group and not an ancestral one."[3] As Karen Radner stressed, however, much of modern scholarship "prefers to see Herodotus's *Medikos Logos* as largely fictitious and cautions against its use as a historical source."[4]

1. Olmstead 1951, 244.
2. Radner 2003. Cf. Potts 2014, 69.
3. Jones 1996, 317, 318.
4. Radner 2013, 454. Cf. Helm 1981.

Herodotus, of course, also famously wrote, "There are many tribes in Persia," and he went on to name the Pasargadae, the Maraphians, and the Maspians, upon whom all the other Persians "hang" (*Hist.* 1.125). The Achaemenids, by which he presumably meant the descent group of the eponymous Achaemenes, were part of the Pasargadae, a "Königshaus" in the words of Hans Heinrich Schaeder.[5] In describing the Achaemenids, Herodotus used the term *phratry* (*phrētrē*; φρατρία), and it is striking that no other social or demographic category discussed in his work was identified in this way. Some years ago, the ancient Greek historian Pietro Vannicelli noted, "*Phrētrē* is generally translated 'clan,' but this translation does not really help in understanding the definition given by Herodotus." Vannicelli went on to note that the *genos*—possibly a descent group, as mentioned above— was a subset of the phratry in normal Greek usage.[6] Lewis Henry Morgan considered the phratry to be "a brotherhood, as the term imports, and a natural growth from the organization into gentes. It is an organic union or association of two or more gentes of the same tribe for common objects."[7] This is actually the opposite of what Herodotus implied when he called the Achaemenid phratry part of the Pasargadae *genos*.[8] Moreover, *genos* was the term used for tribe when Herodotus and Ctesias discussed the Mardoi.[9]

But as Sarre and Herzfeld noted in 1910, the question of clans and tribes in ancient Iran is complicated.[10] They cited the great German Iranologist Friedrich Carl Andreas, who suggested that the record of Darius I's descent given at Nāqš-e Rostām (DNa)—son of Vištāspa, of the Achaemenid clan, a Persian, son of a Persian, an Aryan, of Aryan lineage[11]—was a direct reflection of Avestan social terminology, from family/house (*nmana*), village/clan (*vis-*), and tribe (*zantu-*) to land (*dahyu*).[12] Émile Benveniste and Arthur Christensen both believed this quadripartite division of Iranian patriarchal society was essentially territorial,[13]

5. Schaeder 1936, 748.

6. Vannicelli 2012, 266n29.

7. Morgan 1877, 88.

8. This point was emphasized by Waters (2004, 96). This recalls Herodotus's use of the terms *ethnos* and *genos*, for, as Jones (1996, 315) noted, "an *ethnos* is sometimes a subdivision of the *genos*, and sometimes the contrary." In British anthropological discourse, as Fortes (1953, 25) observed many years ago in discussing unilineal descent groups, "British anthropologists now regularly use the term *lineage* for these descent groups . . . to distinguish them from wider often dispersed divisions of society ordered to the notion of common—but not demonstrable and often mythological—ancestry for which we find it useful to reserve the label *clan*."

9. Andreas 1904, 95. Cf. Herodotus, *Hist.* 1.125; and for Ctesias, see Lenfant 2004, 93–95, 103. On the Mardians, see the long discussion in Potts 2014, 94–99.

10. Sarre and Herzfeld 1910, 16.

11. See Kent 1950, 138: "son of Hystaspes, an Achaemenian, a Persian, son of a Persian, an Aryan, having Aryan lineage." Cf. Lecoq 1997, 219; Schmitt 2009, 100.

12. Sarre and Herzfeld 1910, 16; Meillet 1925, 23.

13. Benveniste 1932, 125; Christensen 1936, 13.

FIGURE 8. Darius I's relief at Bisotun (photo: courtesy of W.F.M. Henkelman).

whereas, for Antoine Meillet, it was political.[14] Andreas, in contrast, believed it was both: *vis* could refer to a territorial entity, in this case the clan's village or habitat, or it "may signify the people themselves."[15]

DARIUS I'S GENEALOGICAL CHARTER

The term Haxāmanišiyā, or Achaemenids, used by Darius, has been called a "Sippenbezeichnung,"[16] or "pro-patronymic."[17] It was used both by Herodotus (*Hist.* 1.125) and Darius I in his Bisotun inscription (DB I §§1–2; see fig. 8). There, the newly minted Persian king traced his descent via Hystaspes, Arsames, Ariaramnes, and Teispes—establishing a link to Cyrus via Teispes—back to the eponymous Achaemenes.

Much has been written over the years on the veracity, or otherwise, of the lineage given by Darius. Pierre Briant, for example, wrote of Darius's insistence, "not without falsification," of his filiation or, more correctly, his descent.[18] One relevant

14. Meillet 1925, 23.

15. Herzfeld 1937, 937.

16. Shayegan 2010, 176n16.

17. Schmitt 2002, 364.

18. Briant 1996, 1:535. Cf. Kent 1946, 212, who speculated "that Ctesias gave . . . [a] falsified account of Cyrus's origin at the request of Artaxerxes II, who was seeking in every way to discredit the line and even the very name of Cyrus." Vallat (1997, 429–30) gave a rather tortured explanation,

point has been largely overlooked in the debate over Darius's claims, however. As Bronislaw Malinowski pointed out, a genealogy should be viewed as "a legal charter rather than an historical record."[19] Echoing this point, A. R. Radcliffe-Brown noted, in 1935, that genealogy is "fundamentally a jural concept."[20] Similarly, as Meyer Fortes stressed, "If there is one thing all recent investigations are agreed upon it is that lineage genealogies are not historically accurate. But they can be understood if they are seen to be the conceptualization of the existing lineage structure viewed as continuing through time and therefore projected backward as pseudo-history."[21] In fact, Paul and Laura Bohannan found the Tiv of northern Nigeria "rearranging their lineage genealogies to bring them into line with changes in the existing pattern of legal and political relations within and between lineages."[22] This certainly reminds one of Darius I and, when read with DB I §§1–2 in mind, the observations of Malinowski, Radcliffe-Brown, Fortes, and the Bohannans strongly suggest that a literal reading of the genealogy of Darius I misses the point, nor does its biological accuracy, or otherwise, bear any relation to its real intent. Darius I's genealogical charter is, as foreshadowed in chapter 1, a record of "arrangement and alignment, in the first place a principle of political design."[23]

DARIUS I'S CHOICE OF XERXES AS HIS SUCCESSOR

As Evelyn Cecil noted in discussing primogeniture in feudal Europe, "For a time, before primogeniture was fully established, a lord had been able to bestow his feud on whichever of his sons he thought proper." Cecil was decidedly of the opinion, however, "that primogeniture in the West has been of the highest political value in averting internal discord and civil war. . . . There is no recorded parallel to the infamies attending some of the Ottoman successions. The Shahs of Persia and earlier Indian princes were scarcely more discriminating than their imperial brothers of Turkey. Unscrupulous family murder commonly inaugurated their reigns."[24]

The issue of primogeniture in royal succession, as opposed to property or titular inheritance, arises in the case of Darius I's choice of his son Xerxes as his designated successor. In 2015 Richard Stoneman discussed this topic at length.[25] His two

---

seeking to harmonize all of the names given in the genealogies of both Darius and Xerxes, but it requires so many unverifiable assumptions that it is hardly credible.

19. Fortes 1953, 27–28, paraphrasing Malinowski 1926, 56.
20. Quoted in Fortes 1953, 28.
21. Fortes 1953, 27.
22. Quoted in Fortes 1953, 27–28.
23. Sahlins 1965, 106.
24. Cecil 1895, 87, 79.
25. Stoneman 2015, 23–26.

main sources, Herodotus (7.2–3) and Justin (2.10.1–10), are largely in agreement. According to Herodotus:

> Before Darius became king, he already had three sons from his earlier wife, the daughter of Gobryas; after he became king, he had four more by Atossa, the daughter of Cyrus. The eldest of the first three was Ariobazanes, and Xerxes of the second family. As they were not from the same mother they were at odds with each other: Ariobazanes claiming that he was the eldest of all the children and that it was customary among all mankind for the eldest to have precedence, while Xerxes claimed that he was the son of the daughter of Cyrus, and it was Cyrus who had established freedom for the Persians.

Justin differs in naming Ariaramnes as the eldest of Darius's first group of children, rather than Ariobazanes, noting that Ariaramnes

> claimed the throne by reason of his age: order of birth and nature itself had established this law among all people. But Xerxes wanted to move the debate, not to the issue of rank, but to the timing of their birth. In his view, Ariaramnes was certainly Darius' first-born, but while Darius was still a *subject*, whereas *he* was the first-born of Darius as king. For that reason, his older brother was entitled to claim the private property which their father had owned, but not the throne; but it was he who was the first child born to his father *after* his accession to the throne. . . . Even were it to be supposed that the two brothers had equal rights because of their father, he would still win out because of his mother and paternal grandfather.[26]

Thus, the justification for Xerxes's succession implied by Justin was his pedigree rather than, as has sometimes been argued, the influence of his mother Atossa.[27] The sources agree in recognizing Darius's second wife, Atossa, as a daughter of Cyrus the Great, whereas Darius I's "earlier wife," as Herodotus put it, was a daughter of Gobryas.[28] I suggest that filiation and descent were the decisive factors in the promotion of Xerxes over Ariobazanes, not the fact that Darius I was king when Xerxes was born but not when Ariobazanes was born. A parallel situation occurred more than two thousand years later in Fath 'Ali Shah's choice of 'Abbas Mirza—his second,[29] third[30] or fourth[31] son, depending on which source one believes[32]—as crown-prince, over his eldest son Mohammad 'Ali Mirza. This has always been explained by the fact that the mother of Mohammad 'Ali Mirza was a Georgian slave, whereas that of 'Abbas Mirza was Asiya Khanom, daughter

26. Quotes taken from Kuhrt 2007, 245–46.

27. On the basis of the Persepolis Fortification texts, Henkelman (2010b) disputed the power and influence of Atossa.

28. She was possibly Apame. See Kuhrt 2007, 173n1 and 245n4.

29. Johnson 1818, 169; von Hammer 1819, 281; Anonymous 1834, 322.

30. Tancoigne 1820, 72.

31. Eichwald 1837, 551; Hasan-e Fasa'i (Busse 1972, 36).

32. An anonymous author (1873, 715, 717) lists him as the firstborn son of Fath 'Ali Shah, but this is contradicted by all other sources.

of Fath ʿAli Khan Devellu, a high-born Qajar whom Fath ʿAli Shah had married at the behest of his uncle and predecessor on the throne, Aqa Mohammad Shah.[33] As James Silk Buckingham wrote in 1830, Fath ʿAli Shah's eldest two sons, Mohamad Vali Mirza and Mohammad ʿAli Mirza, "are the offspring of the king by Georgian women; the third is by a high-born female of the Kujur tribe, and is therefore chosen to succeed the King."[34]

SISIGAMBIS, MOTHER OF DARIUS III

A curious case of kin relations in the late Achaemenid period is afforded by an episode recounted by both Diodorus and Quintus Curtius. *En route* from Susa to Persepolis Alexander's progress was impeded in the mountain territory of the Uxians, whose governor (*praefectus regionis*) Madates/Medates initially put up stiff resistance to the Macedonian advance. Eventually, Alexander was forced to seek refuge in a mountain citadel, from which he only emerged thanks to the intervention of Sisigambis, the mother of Darius III.[35]

Alexander's relationship with Sisigambis is described at length by Quintus Curtius. Under severe pressure, the Uxians appealed to her to use her good offices with Alexander to pardon "both those who had been taken prisoner and those who had surrendered" (*Hist. Alex.* 5.3.15). This personal intervention has led Ali Bahadori, in a recent article on the Achaemenid Empire and what he calls the tribal confederations of southwestern Persia, to assume that both Sisigambis and Madates were Uxians, which made her "an ideal person to negotiate with Alexander."[36] This inference, however, is flatly contradicted by the ancient sources, which show that Sisigambis was a granddaughter of Darius II and probably a daughter of Ostanes/ Uštana, brother of Artaxerxes II, and hence his niece.[37] She was thus a first cousin of Artaxerxes III.[38]

Diodorus (17.5.5) says that Darius III "was the son of Arsanes"; hence, Arsanes was Sisigambis's husband, and "grandson of that Ostanes who was a brother of Artaxerxes, who had been king"—that is, Artaxerxes II. The credit for unraveling the complex filiation and descent of Sisigambis goes to the ancient historian Otto Neuhaus, whose 1902 article on this subject has yet to be superseded.[39] One

---

33. Busse 2011.

34. Buckingham 1830, 415–16n*. Cf. Eichwald 1837, 550n*.

35. On the question of her name, see Badian (2000, 244), who wrote, "We do not know his mother's name. She is consistently called Sisyngambris in Diodorus and usually Sisigambis (with manuscript variants) in Curtius. Neither of these authors is known for accuracy over (especially Persian) names and neither form has found a convincing etymology." For further discussion see also Badian 2015; Yardley and Heckel 1997, 136–37. Justi (1895, 304), s.v. Σισύγγαμβρις, offered no etymology.

36. Bahadori 2017, 173.

37. Neuhaus 1902: 621, 617.

38. For a chart showing Achaemenid filiation, see Briant (1996, 2:793).

39. Neuhaus 1902.

explanation of Sisigambis's efforts on behalf of Madates is given by Quintus Curtius, according to whom Madates was married to Sisigambis's niece, specifically the daughter of her sister "and thus was a near relative of Darius" (*Hist. Alex.* 5.3.12). Diodorus, however, calls Madates a *suggenes* (συγγενής), or kinsman, of Darius III (17.66.4).[40] As anyone can appreciate who has ever delved into the terminology for cousin, nephew, and related kin terms in Greek and Latin or Indo-European languages more broadly,[41] Bradford Welles's identification of Madates as Darius's "cousin" in his Loeb Classical Library translation of Diodorus glossed over and unnecessarily confused their relationship.[42] Rather, the translation "kinsman" is more appropriate given that Madates was not a blood-relation of Darius's but was married to a first cousin of Darius III's and was therefore what we would more accurately call a cousin-by-marriage.[43]

One further point about Sisigambis deserves mention. According to Quintus Curtius (*Hist. Alex.* 10.5.23), she had eighty brothers, all of whom, along with her father, were killed by Artaxerxes III. In the account given by Valerius Maximus (*Memorable Doings and Sayings* 9.2, ext. 7), the deed was even worse, for Artaxerxes III "buried his sister (also his mother-in-law) Atossa alive head downward and killed with darts his uncle along with more than a hundred sons and grandsons, left at his mercy in an empty space; not provoked by any injury but because he saw that they had a great name among the Persians for uprightness and bravery."[44] Justin (10.3.1), however, said, "Possession of the throne was given to Ochus [Artaxerxes III], who, dreading a similar conspiracy [to that perpetrated against his father Artaxerxes II], filled the palace with the blood and dead bodies of his kinsmen and the nobility, being touched with compassion neither for consanguinity, nor sex, nor age, lest, apparently, he should be thought less wicked than his brothers that had meditated parricide."[45] Neuhaus interpreted this mass murder as the politically motivated elimination of all members of the Achaemenid house and court—regardless of age, sex, or degree of relationship—who posed a potential threat to Artaxerxes III's possession of the throne,[46] arguing persuasively that all three accounts reported on one and the same event.[47] The only divergence

---

40. For the different uses of this term, see the discussion in Briant (1996, 1:321–22).

41. Szemerényi 1977, 166–69.

42. See Welles 1963, 309.

43. Waterfield 2019, 461: "Madetes (or Madates) was not just a Kinsman in the honorary sense, but was married to the daughter of the sister of Darius' mother."

44. Cf. Frémion and Soulerin 1834, 255; Neuhaus 1902, 621.

45. Translation from Watson 1853.

46. Neuhaus 1902, 610: "Bekanntlich leitete der Grosskönig Artaxerxes III Ochos seine Regierung durch ein grausiges Blutbad ein, indem er alle Mitglieder des Achämenidengeschlechtes und des Hofes, von denen er in irgend einer Weise Gefahr für den Bestandt seiner Herrschaft befürchten zu müssen glaubte, ohne Rücksicht auf Blutsverwandtschaft, Alter und Geschlecht abschlachten liess."

47. Hall (1989, 188) and Thomas (2018, 69–70n374) stress that although Greek readers would have been shocked by such events, they were familiar with comparable ones in the mythical history of Hellas.

in the accounts concerns the figure of eighty brothers of Sisigambis, according to Quintus Curtius, whereas Valerius Maximus wrote of more than one hundred children and grandchildren of Sisigambis's father. The numbers here are impressive, and we should note that Justin also says that Artaxerxes II had 118 sons, three by "lawful wedlock" and 115 by his concubines (Justin 10.1.1).

Although these numbers may seem wildly exaggerated to twenty-first-century readers, data from the Qajar period show that they are perfectly plausible. Fath 'Ali Shah, for example, had four legitimate wives and 154 secondary wives who bore him a total of 265 children, 159 of whom died in infancy and 106 of whom reached maturity. Six of these predeceased him, leaving him with one hundred children—fifty-five sons and forty five daughters—at the time of his death.[48] As for orchestrating the murder of eighty or one hundred potential rivals, it should be remembered that in 1725, after the flight of Tahmasp Mirza (later Tahmasp II), and the death of Shah Soltan Hoseyn, the Afghan ruler Mahmud had, by some accounts, no fewer than three hundred Safavid nobles and their children or, according to others, 105 nobles, as well as three uncles and seven nephews of Shah Soltan Hoseyn murdered in a single event,[49] thereby almost entirely extinguishing the Safavid line.

PREFERENTIAL MARRIAGE AMONG THE ACHAEMENIDS

Some years ago, the ancient historian Maria Brosius declared that "Persian kings . . . established their connections with the Persian nobility through a deliberate marriage policy," but she remained vague on how this was actually effected.[50] By contrast, in a study published more than thirty years ago on kinship in the early Achaemenid period, Clarisse Herrenschmidt identified several cases of preferential marriage involving both cross-cousins and parallel-cousins.[51]

Chronologically, the earliest case adduced by Herrenschmidt was the alleged cross-cousin, mother's brother's daughter's marriage between Cyrus the Great's son and heir, Cambyses, and his matrilateral cousin Phaidyme (*Hist.* 3.68), the daughter of Cambyses's maternal uncle Otanes—that is, his mother Cassandane's brother. The problem here is that this Otanes was almost certainly not the brother of Cyrus's wife Cassandane. Rather, Herodotus seems to have confused the identities of several homonymous Otanes. For although he says that Cyrus's wife Cassandane was the daughter of the Achaemenid Pharnaspes (*Hist.* 2.1; 3.2) and that Pharnaspes, in birth and wealth the equal of the foremost Persians, also had a son named Otanes (*Hist.* 3.68), the Bisotun inscription (DB IV §68) identifies Otanes's

48. Anonymous 1873, 714.

49. Lockhart 1958, 198; Potts 2022b, 1:34, 71 [three hundred nobles and their children], 77, 78 [105 nobles slain, three uncles of Shah Hoseyn and seven of his nephews], 294n750.

50. Brosius 2010. Cf. Bigwood 2009, 331n114.

51. Herrenschmidt 1987.

father as Thukhra.[52] Moreover, other sources, such as Ctesias (F 9 §§1–2), identify Cambyses's mother not as Cassandane but as Amytis, a daughter of the Mede
Astyages,[53] while Deinon and Lyceas of Naucratis (Athenaeus, *Deipnsophistae*
13.560e–f = Deinon F 11 = Lyceas FGH 613 F 1) identify her as an Egyptian princess
named Neitetis.[54]

The second cross-cousin marriage to which Herrenschmidt drew attention
appears genuine. This involved Mardonius, the son of Gobryas (Herodotus, *Hist.*
3.70; DB IV §68), and Artozostre, the daughter of Darius I (*Hist.* 6.43)[55] by an
unnamed wife.[56] Gobryas was a staunch ally of Darius and his brother-in-law. He
was married to an unnamed sister of Darius. In Herrenschmidt's opinion, "there
is every reason to think that for the Persians who reported these marriages to
Herodotus, they were highly significant."[57] At one level, this is certainly true. But
Herrenschmidt neglected to point out what a more recent paper by John Hyland
explores—namely, the marriages of Gobryas with Darius I's sister (Herodotus, *Hist.*
7.5.1) and of Darius I himself with his brother-in-law Gobryas's daughter (Herodotus, *Hist.* 7.2.2). These marriages, Hyland argues, reflected "the probable agency of
Hystaspes, Darius' father, in arranging both unions before Darius emerged as a
contender for the throne," rather than an attempt by Darius himself, after becom-
ing king, to consolidate power through marriage. Thus, Hyland sees the marriage
in the context of "the aspirations of Hystaspes and Gobryas under Cambyses."[58] But
although Hyland noted that the marriage of Mardonius and Artozostre "extended
their familial connection in the next generation,"[59] he neglected to point out that
this was a classic cross-cousin marriage. From the standpoint of Mardonius, this
was a marriage with his mother's (unnamed) brother's (Darius I) daughter (Artozostre); while from Artozostre's perspective, it was a marriage with her father's
(Darius I) sister's (unnamed) son (Mardonius). Moreover, in highlighting what
he called the aspirations of Hystaspes and Gobryas, Hyland overlooked one of the
most salient features of marriage as "a systematically organised affair which forms
part of a series of contractual obligations between two groups," as opposed to a
marriage representing "the whims of two persons acting as private individuals," to
cite Edmund Leach. "The social groups which 'arrange' such a marriage between
themselves are, in almost all societies, of essentially the same kind. The core of
such a group is composed of the adult males of a kin group all resident in one
place." More precisely, Leach argued that, whereas he did not wish to imply that

---

52. Cf. Briant 1996, 1:123 and 147. See Scott 2005, 492–93 on the seven Otanes mentioned by
Herodotus and DB and the likelihood that two or more of these references apply to the same person.

53. Lenfant 2004, 109.

54. See the discussion in Henkelman 2011, 596n61.

55. In PFa 5, dated to March 498 BC, she received flour rations at several places in western Fars,
viz. Liduma, Bessitme, and Kurdušum. See Kuhrt 2007, 599n4.

56. Scott 2005, 492.

57. Herrenschmidt 1987, 54.

58. Hyland 2018, 31, 32.

59. Hyland 2018, 33.

"women have no part to play in the arrangement of a marriage or that remotely situated kinsfolk are wholly ignored," he believed that "the corporate group of persons who have the most decisive say in bringing about an arranged marriage is always a group of co-resident males representing, as a rule, three genealogical generations, namely: the old men or grandfathers, the normal adults or fathers, and the young adults or sons," and in normal circumstances, membership in such a group "is defined by descent as well as residence."[60]

Unfortunately, the many lacunae in our genealogical information on the Persian nobility render too much speculation on the details of such a hypothetical arrangement pointless. We do not know, for example, whether any kinship ties existed between Hystaspes or his father, Arsames, and Gobryas and his father, Mardonius (the elder), but the fundamental point made by Hyland still stands with respect to the participants in the marriages of Darius, Mardonius, and Artozostre—namely, that this was less about them than it was about their elders and the alliances they wished to forge by employing, in the case of Mardonius and Artozostre, the vehicle of cross-cousin marriage.

Turning to parallel-cousin alliances, we find that although Herrenschmidt found these to be extremely rare in the totality of Greek literature concerned with the Achaemenid Persians, she did identify one within the Achaemenid descent group: the marriage between Darius,[61] eldest son of Xerxes (and thus a grandson of Darius I) and Amestris, to Artaynte (Ἀρταΰντη),[62] a daughter of Xerxes's younger brother—that is, Darius's paternal uncle, Masistes (Μασίστης) and his unnamed wife (Herodotus, *Hist.* 9.108.1).[63] The melodramatic novella built around this marriage packs much more of a punch than a simple kinship diagram of a parallel-cousin union might suggest and has all of the suspense of an opera. Indeed, Drew Griffith called the story "a quasi-Sophoclean tragedy of error."[64]

The story runs as follows: although married to Amestris, Xerxes fell in love with his brother Masistes's unnamed wife.[65] Out of respect for his brother, Xerxes

---

60. Leach 1951, 24.

61. For Darius, who never succeeded his murdered father, Xerxes, but whose reign was instead usurped by his brother Artaxerxes I, see Schmitt 2011b. Griffith (2011, 310) thus erred when he identified him as "the future Darius II."

62. For the name, see Schmitt 2011a, 114, §72.

63. Herrenschmidt 1987: 54.

64. Griffith 2011, 312. The story was, in fact, dramatized; see, e.g., Jodrell's (1822) *The Persian Heroine: A Tragedy.*

65. Larson (2006, 241–42) noted:

Within the social context surrounding respectable women's names . . . Herodotus' omission of the names for Kandaules' and Masistes' wives emphasizes anxiety for their personal and familial *aidôs*. This interpretation accords with two of the interrelated reasons Herodotus gives for purposeful omission of names elsewhere in his work: namely, that his *logos* requires the omission and that anonymity marks the unnamed with respect. . . . Finally, by omitting the names of respectable women from . . . narratives concerning the abuse of tyranny, Herodotus not only exculpates these women from direct blame, but further implicates the male protagonists as responsible parties in their own destruction and the downfall of their dynasties.

accepted the refusal of his advances by Masistes's wife. As a kind of recompense, however, he married off his son Darius to Masistes's daughter Artaynte as a way of maintaining access to the object of his desire. Thus, this was not a parallel-cousin marriage with a "rational" political or economic motivation; rather, it was an amorous one, albeit involving Xerxes's *amour* rather than that of his son Darius.[66] While sharing his palace at Susa with Darius and Artaynte, Xerxes lusted after his daughter-in-law, and they began a relationship. Meanwhile, Xerxes received a beautiful robe from his wife, Amestris, who had woven it herself. Unfortunately, he made the mistake of appearing in it when next he saw Artaynte. Being "pleased with her," Xerxes swore a "blind oath,"[67] offering Artaynte anything she asked for. When she demanded the very robe Amestris had given him, Xerxes became fearful lest her being seen wearing it would provide proof of his affair. Consequently, Xerxes offered Artaynte cities, gold beyond measure, and an army for her own command. Still, she insisted on having the robe.[68]

Learning of this, Amestris became convinced that this was not Artaynte's doing but her mother's, and on Xerxes's birthday, when the king granted gifts to those who petitioned him, Amestris asked for Artaynte's mother. Xerxes, as Herodotus says, "nodded down"[69]—that is, acquiesced—and the unfortunate woman was borne away (fig. 9). Then, with the help of some of Xerxes's guards, Amestris "cut off the woman's breasts and threw them to dogs, and her nose and ears and lips likewise, and cut out her tongue, and sent her home thus cruelly used" (Herodotus, *Hist.* 9.112).

Anticipating the evil that Amestris might perpetrate, Xerxes tried to convince his brother Masistes to abandon his wife, even offering him one of his own daughters in marriage. Masistes, however, refused, replying, "What wicked word do you say to me, bidding me divorce my wife, who gave me sons and daughters, one of whom you married to your son, and who besides is very much to my mind—you bid me divorce her and marry your daughter?" (Herodotus, *Hist.* 9.113).[70] Sensing that something terrible was going to transpire, Masistes then rushed home and, after finding the mutilated body of his wife, he immediately set out with his sons for Bactria, where he hoped to raise a rebellion against his brother. Xerxes, however, had him pursued and killed. The unnamed, mutilated mother of Artaynte, one assumes, died from her wounds. Herodotus, however, never revealed the fate of Artaynte herself.

---

66. For an excellent discussion of the entire episode, see Müller (2006, 290–300). Cf. the long treatment in Hazewindus (2004, 83–128).

67. Fletcher 2012, 31.

68. Sancisi-Weerdenburg (1983, 29) cites Plutarch, *Artaxerxes* 5.2, on the prohibition against anyone but the king wearing the royal robe and suggests that the robe = kingship in this instance, for "the robe is surrounded by emotional feelings that completely hide its original meaning."

69. Griffith 2011: 310.

70. Cf. the discussion of this and other dramatic devices in Lang (1984, 46).

Mishandeling van de Gemalinne van MAZISTES, Schoondogter des Persischen Koning DARIUS.

FIGURE 9. The mistreatment of Masistes' wife (*Mishandeling van de gemalinne van Mazistes, schoondogter des Persischen Koning Darius*, by Jan Luyken, 1699. Etching on paper. H: 193 mm; W: 154 mm. Rijksmuseum, RP-P-OB-44.754. https://creativecommons.org/publicdomain/zero/1.0/deed.en.

Unsurprisingly, commentators have read this story in many different ways. Although Heleen Sancisi-Weerdenburg proposed that it "originates from Persian oral tradition," Drew Griffith suggested that it was inspired by the myth of Zeus and Semele.[71] Erwin Wolff placed it in the genre of "harem love stories,"

71. Sancisi-Weerdenburg 1983, 28; Griffith 2011, 311.

whereas other scholars have compared it with the tales of Salomé and Esther.[72] The whole episode has been understood as a dire portent of Xerxes's ultimate downfall via assassination, a deed committed by Artabanus, the commander of his bodyguard, but pinned on Xerxes's son Darius, for which the latter paid with his life after his younger brother Artaxerxes I found out and killed him, according to Ctesias.[73] Herrenschmidt noted that "the particular arrangement of this marriage and the bloody conclusion [of the story] might lead to the thought that patrilateral parallel-cousin marriages were forbidden." Although she rejected this viewpoint, she nonetheless thought that, unlike cross-cousin marriages, parallel-cousin unions were decried by the lineages that were injured by them; hence, the story of Masistes would be, if not a myth serving to illustrate the interdiction of parallel-cousin marriages, then at least a stark illustration of the evils brought about by the practice.[74]

Many commentators have suggested that the story "The King's Amour, or the Death of Masistes," as Reginald Walter Macan called it,[75] is an embellished tale of lust and revenge intertwined with a genuine attempt on Masistes's part to raise a rebellion in Bactria and overthrow his corrupt brother Xerxes in the aftermath of the Persian defeat at Salamis.[76] Although Artaynte herself disappears from view just as things start to get violent, we should not lose sight of the fact that, from the perspective of young Darius, Artaynte was his father's (Xerxes) brother's (Masistes) daughter—that is, his parallel-cousin.

Parallel-cousins and parallel-cousin marriages have been the subject of many studies. For example, in his examination of parallel-cousin marriage in Iraqi Kurdish society, the Norwegian anthropologist Fredrik Barth noted that parallel-cousins paid a reduced brideprice compared to more distant kin or unrelated marriage partners, leading him to ask, "What are the advantages gained in this system by giving one's daughter to a brother's son which compensate one for the loss of the brideprice?"[77] The compensation, he decided, was first and foremost political, since Kurdish villages were "characterized by a constant struggle for political power on the part of a majority of the adult men, at times even women," and "a man can expect political support only from his agnatic relatives, those who by descent belong to his political sub-section," which segments "consist primarily of brothers, sons, and brother's sons. . . . If a man alienates his nephews by refusing them their traditional rights, he loses their political support. If he, on the other

72. Wolff 1964, 55.

73. Jacoby Frg. III.C. p. 464, frgs. 13–14, §§33–34. See Lenfant 2004, 127; Schmitt 2011b. In the alternative account given by Aristotle (*Politica* 1311b), Artabanus killed Darius and then Xerxes.

74. Herrenschmidt 1987, 55 and note 2.

75. Macan 1908, 812.

76. See the discussion in Müller (2006, 297–99). On the impact of Xerxes's assassination on the young Herodotus in 465 BC, see Wolff (1964, 53–54).

77. Barth 1986, 168.

hand, gives them his daughters in marriage, the ties are reinforced and lineage solidarity maintained."[78]

Decades later, the Dutch scholar Martin van Bruinessen stressed that in Kurd-istan, "there is a clear preference for marriage with the father's brother's daugh-ter. . . . In fact, a girl's father's brother's son," like Darius, son of Xerxes, "has the theoretical right to deny her to anyone else. . . . And if a father's brother's son"—think Darius—"proposes, the girl's father"—think Masistes—"finds it difficult, if not impossible to refuse him. . . . It is evident that a consistent practice of this marriage type leads to extreme segmentariness. . . . Whereas cross-cousin mar-riage . . . cements multiple relationships between lineages, the strict endogamy resulting from father's brother's daughter marriage only enhances the segmentary character of the lineages. . . . The lineages are completely isolated; there are no affinal relations to soften the potential conflicts between them."[79] Herrenschmidt's assessment of the Masistes story as an illustration of the evils of parallel-cousin marriage ignored all of these important considerations, and the Kurdish example suggests that parallel-cousin marriage is a tried and true strategy deployed to forge and strengthen political alliances.

It may be argued, of course, that the ultimate tragedies in the story of Xerxes, Darius, Amestris, Masistes, his wife, and Artaynte play out on a very different plane: Xerxes brought about the destruction of his brother's family and was even-tually murdered; Masistes and his sons attempted to launch a rebellion and were all killed. The tragedy of brother-to-brother rivalry is, however, somehow banal in the context of Iranian history when, as noted earlier, Safavid, Qajar, Arsacid,[80] and of course Achaemenid, holders or contenders for the throne, did not hesi-tate to eliminate their rivals by the dozens, or the hundreds, although this usually occurred prior to or in the process of consolidating power. Perhaps the significance of parallel-cousin marriage, in the case of Darius and Artaynte, lies rather in the strengthening effect it would have had, but for Xerxes's *eros*, in bolstering a seg-mentary lineage and shoring it up against potential threats from not-quite-so-near kin. After all, as the Dhund in Pakistan said, "Marriage with *dādā potrī* (FBD) [father's brother's daughter] is a good marriage—if my brother has a daughter and I have a son, I will always ask for her in marriage before I ask outside. With this kind of marriage everyone is known to everyone else; I know if my brother and his daughter are good people or not and so with this marriage there is no trouble

---

78. Barth 1986, 393.

79. Bruinessen 1992, 72.

80. Thus, Tacitus, *Annals* 11.8: "Parthia was in a distracted state, the dispute about the sovereignty having withdrawn all attention from minor matters. For the Parthian King Gotarzes, among other cruelties, had put to death his brother Artabanus, as well as his wife and son"; and *Annals* 12.10: "the tyranny of Gotarzes . . . was intolerable alike to the nobles and to the people. He had slain his broth-ers, his relations, near and distant, nay, even their pregnant wives and little children. A sluggard at home, unfortunate in war, his cruelty was but a cloak for cowardice." Cf. Karras-Klapproth 1988, 39.

afterwards. In a similar vein FBD marriage is seen as fostering good relations between two brothers."[81]

Yet another issue raised in this story is that of a girl's marriage with her paternal uncle. According to Herodotus (*Hist.* 9.111), Xerxes demanded of his brother, "you must live no longer with her who is now your wife. I give you my daughter in her place; take her for your own; but put away the wife that you have, for it is not my will that you should have her." This was, of course, a measure of extreme desperation on Xerxes's part, an offer made to avert what he rightly sensed would be a catastrophe, both for himself and his brother's family.

And what of the phenomenon of "niece marriage"? Two of Darius I's nieces—the unnamed daughter of his sister and brother-in-law Gobryas, and Phratagune, the only child of his brother Artanes—became his wives.[82] According to Herodotus (*Hist.* 7.224), "this Artanes was brother to king Darius, and son of Hystaspes who was the son of Arsames; and when he gave his daughter in marriage to Darius he dowered her with the whole wealth of his house, she being his only child." In the so-called Levitical Degrees which hold a prominent place in Rabbinical Law, such marriages were not only permitted but considered meritorious, the only caveat here being that they usually involved the marriage of a brother with his sister's daughter rather than a brother with his brother's daughter, as proposed by Xerxes to Masistes.[83] There is a memorable scene in Robert Graves's *Claudius the God* in which Vitellius recommends that Claudius marry his niece Agrippinilla. Claudius protests, "But, Vitellius, she's my niece. I can't marry my niece, can I?" Vitellius replies by saying he'd be happy to approach the Senate for their consent and continues: "And why shouldn't uncle and niece marry? The Parthians do it, and theirs is a very old civilization. And in the Herod family there have been more marriages between uncle and niece than any other sort." This gives Claudius pause, and he replies, "That's right. . . . Herodias married her uncle Philip, and then deserted him and ran off with her uncle Antipas. And Herod Agrippa's daughter Berenice married her uncle Herod Pollio, King of Chalcis. . . . Why shouldn't the Cæsars be as free as the Herods." To this Vitellius says that in contrast to brother-sister incest, "it may well be that our very earliest ancestors allowed uncle and niece to marry; because there is nowhere any disgust expressed in ancient classical literature for Pluto's marriage with his niece Proserpine."[84]

Clarisse Herrenschmidt suggested that the uncle-niece marriage arranged by Artanes between his daughter Phratagune and his brother Darius was intended to conserve Artanes's wealth within the narrowest confines of the Achaemenid dynasty, since a cross-cousin marriage would have placed that wealth in the hands

81. Donnan 1988, 128.
82. Scott 2005, 492.
83. Zschokke 1883, 50. Cf. Michaelis 1793, 310, §117.
84. Graves 1935, 480.

of the spouse's family.[85] But such a basic economic argument was not among those traditionally considered by biblical and Talmudic scholars. In the East, according to Johann David Michaelis, the relationship with the brother's daughter was not considered as close as that with the father's sister, a point underscored by the fact that in Muslim societies, relatives who could see an aunt unveiled could only see a daughter veiled.[86] In his famous study of ancient Israel, Heinrich Ewald contended that in contrast to Roman society, a father's reputation was less injured by a marriage between an uncle and a niece than by an aunt and a nephew.[87] None of these justifications is particularly satisfying; and, as Moses Mielziner noted in 1901, whereas Roman Catholic canon law, as well as English statutory law, prohibited uncle-niece marriage, "in other Protestant States of Europe such marriages are allowed. In some of the States of this country [the United States]," he wrote, "as in Ohio, Illinois, Michigan and Louisiana, they are unlawful by statute,"[88] but elsewhere they were not prohibited. In fact, whereas uncle-niece and aunt-nephew marriages are today prohibited and considered a class E felony, such marriages were legal in New York until 1893.[89]

The renowned Scottish anthropologist and folklorist Sir James G. Frazer discussed uncle-niece marriage among the Hovas of Madagascar:

> The king generally married, not his sister, but her daughter, his niece, and the children whom he had by her were the heirs to the throne in virtue of a twofold right, since they inherited the blood royal from their mothers as well as from their fathers. It is possible that a similar motive may explain the leave granted by some peoples to an uncle to marry his niece in the case in which the niece is his sister's daughter. Such a marriage would serve the same purpose as marriage with a sister and would be less shocking to traditional sentiment.[90]

No mention is made here of a king marrying a brother's daughter.

INCESTUOUS MARRIAGE
IN THE ACHAEMENID PERIOD?

The matter of uncle-niece marriage, which was sanctioned in the Bible but deemed too close for comfort in the late nineteenth-century West, brings us to the broader topic of close-kin or incestuous marriage. In 1645 the first edition of Pierre Du Ryer's French translation of Herodotus's *Histories* appeared; and, unsurprisingly, it soon became a source for enterprising authors in search of new material. One writer who delved into Herodotus's portrayal of the Persian past was the young

---

85. Herrenschmidt 1987, 56.

86. Michaelis (1786, 320) decided that if Mosaic law did not expressly forbid a type of marriage, it was deemed acceptable. Cf. Michaelis 1793, 312, §117.

87. Ewald 1866, 262.

88. Mielziner 1901, 40.

89. Harris et al. 2018, 177.

90. Frazer 1935, 525–26.

poet and playwright Philippe Quinault (1635–88). Two plays with strong roots in Herodotus appeared in 1656: *La mort de Cyrus* and *Le mariage de Cambise* were identified by their author as a "tragedy" and a "tragi-comedy" (figs. 10, 11).[91]

Discussing Quinault's dramatic works, William Brooks suggested that "Quinault takes from his source a few ideas and names—Gobryas, Prexaspes, Megabyzus, Otanes, Phaedima, Parmys—and invents the rest, including infant substitution and the salacious thrill of possible incest."[92] Thus, early in act 2, scene 1 of *Le mariage de Cambise*, Atossa, the historical Udusana of the Persepolis Fortification texts[93]—whom we know was a daughter of Cyrus and therefore a sister or half-sister of Cambyses—tells her sister Aristonne (obviously a name recalling Artystone, the historical Irtaštuna)[94] that regardless of how charming the crown might be in her eyes, she dare not touch the hand that offered it. Although Cambyses was so dear to her that he could not please her more, to call him lover was repugnant to her and to the designation of him as brother; and as attractive as marriage with him might seem to be, it must be odious, an insult to nature, an offense to the gods.[95]

In Cambyses's case, it would seem, the incest theme was not Quinault's invention. Nevertheless, scholars have debated long and hard whether it was Herodotus's. According to him, Cambyses had not one but two incestuous relationships with siblings, although the veracity of his claims has been questioned. First, as noted above, we are not certain who Cambyses's mother was. She may have been Cassandane (Herodotus, *Hist.* 3.2), Amytis,[96] or Neitetis. Herodotus called Cyrus's Egyptian wife "the new-comer from Egypt" and alleged that, as an Egyptian interloper, her presence prompted Cambyses's decision, when he was only ten years old, to one day conquer Egypt, by way of avenging his own mother Cassandane's honor (*Hist.* 3.3).[97] Second, neither Herodotus (*Hist.* 3.88, 7.69) nor any other source reveals who the mother or mothers of Atossa and the unidentified second daughter[98] of Cyrus were, who were said to have married Cambyses.[99] Herodotus

---

91. Parfaict 1746, 196; Fieux 1780, 287.

92. Brooks 2009, 181. Cf. Gros 1970, 283–84, who also commented on Quinault's "deformation of history."

93. Hallock 1969, 117; Henkelman and Kleber 2007, 169. Both later married Darius I, but it was the younger sister, Irtaštuna/Artystone, not Udusana/Atossa, who "was indeed considered as leading in 'Teispid affairs,'" a point underscored by the importance of her son Iršama/Arshama. See Henkelman 2010a, 703.

94. See Henkelman 2010a.

95. Quinault 1659, 17.

96. Lenfant 2004, 118, F13.11.

97. Bichler 2001, 210.

98. As Lenfant (2019, 34) noted, "For his part, Ctesias mentions Rhoxane as a wife who gave birth to a child without a head (F 13.14). The reader does not know whether that woman is meant to equate with one of the sisters mentioned by Herodotus, but it is worth noting that she is the only wife of Cambyses to be mentioned in Ctesias' fragments."

99. Von Cleß 1864, 49.

FIGURE 10. Title page of Philippe Quinault, *La mort de Cyrus,* by Caspar Luyken, 1697. Etching on paper. H: 119 mm; W: 66 mm. Rijksmuseum, RP-P-1896-A-19368-1118. https://creativecommons.org/publicdomain /zero/1.0/deed.en.

FIGURE 11. Title page of Philippe Quinault, *Le mariage de Cambise,*
by Caspar Luyken, 1697. Etching on paper. H: 118 mm; W: 66 mm.
Rijksmuseum, RP-P-1896-A-19368-1119. https://creativecommons.org
/publicdomain/zero/1.0/deed.en.

was explicit in asserting that the younger of the two sisters whom Cambyses married, and whom he killed in Egypt, was a full sister (*Hist.* 3.31).[100] The fact that Atossa was not identified in this way may be at the root of the belief, sometimes found in the literature, that she was a half-sister, but this remains conjectural.[101] Nor is there any reason to suggest, as the Lutheran theologian Christian Matthiae did in 1699, that Atossa and her unnamed sister were coerced into marrying Cambyses.[102]

Although few commentators on Herodotus and the Persian empire have questioned the accusation of royal incest on the part of Cambyses, this has changed in recent years. Maria Brosius, for example, wrote:

> Against the accusation of Cambyses' incestuous marriages stands Herodotus' own statement that Cambyses was married to Otanes' daughter Phaidyme, as well as Ctesias' reference to a wife named Roxane (FGrH 688 F13), whom he does not identify as a sister. Furthermore, the fact that the accusation of incest is listed in a series of sacrilegious acts committed by Cambyses, all of which are to emphasize his insanity and hubris, should caution against their existence. They derived from a common Egyptian source hostile to Cambyses, and some of these atrocities, such as the killing of the Apis bull, have been proved to be untrue.[103]

Cambyses's alleged incest could, of course, be a case of slander, but if genuine, it would hardly be unique. For example, according to the *Karlamagnus Saga*, Charlemagne had an illicit liaison with his sister Gille and failed to confess this to the Abbot Egidius until the angel Gabriel brought a letter from God exposing it and ordering Charlemagne to give his sister to Milon d'Anglers in marriage. Charlemagne made Milon the Duke of Brittany, and seven months later Gille gave birth to Charlemagne's illegitimate son, the future hero Roland.[104] Other medieval sources simply say that Charlemagne suffered under the weight of a great, unnamed sin all his life.[105]

Rather than dismissing Herodotus's account of Cambyses's two incestuous alliances,[106] some scholars have tried to understand them in an Egyptian or ancient Iranian cultural context. For example, in 1866, Adolf Rapp suggested that, in making Cambyses the creator of the tradition of brother-sister marriage among

---

100. For an Egyptian perspective on this episode, see Griffith 2009.

101. Wiesehöfer 2001, 84; Henkelman and Kleber 2007, 169; Binder 2008, 310; Bigwood 2009, 323. Michaelis (1786, 169) saw a major distinction in Cambyses's behavior. Herodotus qualified Cambyses's unnamed wife as his sister via both of his parents—that is, not a half-sister. When Herodotus said that, prior to Cambyses, marriage with the sister was an unknown custom among the Persians, Michaelis felt he only meant marriage with a full sister but that marriage with half-sisters had occurred.

102. Matthiae 1699, 113.

103. Brosius 2010. Cf. Hoffmann 1981, 179–80; Posener 1936, 30–47 and 171.

104. Paris 1865, 378–80.

105. Farnsworth 1913, 213–14.

106. Thus, as Bigwood (2009, 323) queried, "Even if we largely disbelieve Herodotus' account, does this mean that no part of it is based on what actually happened? . . . Likewise, we should not automatically reject Cambyses' second sister-marriage as wholly untrue."

the Persians, Herodotus was trying to show that this was a component of the Persians' Zoroastrianism,[107] and in 1879 Philip Keiper proposed that Herodotus was simply trying to fix the practice in space and time for his audience.[108] Wilhelm Geiger, however, attributed Cambyses's incestuous marriages to the fact that he wished to keep the royal blood pure from admixture with other families,[109] a view later expressed by Franz Cumont as well.[110] In 1956, K. M. T. Atkinson argued that Cambyses's marriage to his unnamed full sister, "whom he took with him to Egypt," was "in accordance with Egyptian royal tradition but by no means in accordance with Persian."[111] Citing Yima's incestuous relationship with his twin sister, Yimāk, in *Bundahišn* 23.1, Hoffmann and Vorbichler suggested that sibling marriage was a pre-Zoroastrian religious act unappreciated by Herodotus's Greek audience.[112] In marrying his sister, Cambyses, they argued, was mirroring the mythological act of Yima, the first man, and his sister.[113] An entirely speculative scenario was envisaged by Herrenschmidt, who suggested that brother-sister marriage in the Persian royal family indicated a reluctance to engage in the normal, exogamous exchange of women and might reflect friction between the Teispids and other noble families.[114]

The German ancient historian Ernst Kornemann, in contrast, was much more interested in, why, among all Indo-European-speaking peoples, the Persians, at least the royal house, followed a pattern of explicit endogamy, in contrast to the Romans, who strictly rejected it? He concluded that such a practice was a holdover from the pre-Indo-European and pre-Semitic population that had left a memory of sibling marriage in the mythology of various peoples living around the Mediterranean, a practice perpetuated only by the Persians and Egyptians.[115] Ernst Herzfeld entertained similar views. What he termed "the endogamy of the Achaemenids" was not an ancient Iranian practice, he claimed, but rather an inheritance from the region's "Ureinwohnern" or aboriginal population—that is, the Elamites, who practiced unbridled brother-sister marriage, according to F. W. König, as discussed (and debunked) in chapter 3.[116]

107. Rapp 1866, 112.

108. Keiper 1879, 15.

109. Geiger 1882, 246. Cf. Sanjana 1888, 99–100n2.

110. Cumont 1924, 61.

111. Atkinson 1956, 176. Cf. Grätz 2004, 227n66. Note that Cambyses also adopted an Egyptian throne name. See Posener 1936, 12.

112. Carnoy 1917, 315. Cf. the discussion in Skjærvø 2012 and the literature cited there. It is not mentioned in the Avesta and is consider "another stock argument for brother-and-sister marriage." See Gray 1915, 457n3.

113. Hoffmann and Vorbichler 1980, 96; Hoffmann 1981, 189–90. Cf. Prášek 1913, 6. For an exhaustive review of creation myths involving brother-sister incest see Moore (1964, 1310).

114. Herrenschmidt 1987, 57.

115. Kornemann 1925, 356.

116. Herzfeld 1938a, 255. Cf. Herrenschmidt 1987, 58.

My own inclination is rather to try to understand the rare but well-attested practice of royal brother-sister marriage in a broader context. As with cross-cousin and parallel-cousin marriage, or succession to high office by a ruler's sister's son, the anthropological literature has much to contribute to a better understanding of brother-sister marriage. In 1929, the British anthropologist Brenda Z. Seligman suggested that the brother-sister incest taboo "not only prevents rivalry between brother and brother and between sister and sister, but it removes a second sphere of rivalry between father and son," thereby minimizing the risk of disharmony, fission, and violent conflict in a family.[117] According to Reo Franklin Fortune's alliance-based approach to incest,[118] the prohibition "is adopted not because of its internal value to the family, but because the external value of the marriage alliance is essential to social structure."[119] Seligman rejected this logic, however, arguing that "rather than providing a new theory of incest, Fortune shows a principle for the retention of its laws and offers a sociological basis for exceptions. It would seem that society tolerates incest when the social structure has nothing to gain from its prohibition. This, however, is only partially true. Supernatural sanction has come to aid the enforcement of the law, and does not easily fade as soon as the social structure has no need for it." In fact, as Seligman stressed, in most non-Western societies "no punishment is prescribed" in cases of incest. Rather, incest triggered what she called a "supernatural sanction" that brought about "disease or death," the latter of which often took the form of suicide.[120] Although neither Herodotus nor Seligman cited Cambyses as a case in point, after reading this last statement by Seligman, I could not help but think that, for medieval and later readers of Herodotus, Cambyses's childlessness, alleged madness,[121] and early death all constitute powerful arguments for seeing divine sanction as the ultimate result of his incestuous behavior.

But another perspective, raised by James Frazer (1854–1941) of *Golden Bough* fame, is also relevant. In discussing the Banyoro, a Bantu-speaking group located near Lake Albert on the present-day border of Uganda and the Democratic Republic of Congo, Frazer noted: "To the rule of exogamy observed by the totemic clans of the Banyoro there was one remarkable exception. Princes might cohabit with princesses and have children by them, though in such cases the couple necessarily belonged to the same totemic clan. . . . However, this cohabitation was not marriage." Citing John Roscoe, Frazer continued:

117. Seligman 1929, 246.
118. See Tylor 1889, 266–68; Leavitt 2013, 46. In fact, although Tylor is seen as providing an alliance-oriented refutation of the incest taboo, he was actually contrasting the virtues of exogamy over endogamy. Endogamy does not necessarily equate to incest.
119. Seligman 1935, 90.
120. Seligman 1935, 90–92.
121. McPhee 2018.

The rule . . . was for princes and princesses to live together promiscuously and not to regard each other as husband and wife, though the king might take a princess and keep her in his enclosure. He might even cohabit thus with his full sister and beget children by her. . . . Similarly we . . . find that among the Bahima the princes were allowed to marry their own sisters. What is the reason for these remarkable anomalies? . . . A simple and highly probable explanation of the marriage of a king or chief with his sister was long ago suggested by J. F. McLennan. Under a system of mother-kin a man's heirs are his sister's sons, and, accordingly, where that system prevails, it is the king's sister's son, not his own son, who succeeds him on the throne. . . . According to immemorial tradition a king's heirs were his sister's sons; hence, if he only married his sister, her sons would also be his; the system of maternal descent would be combined with paternal descent; time-honoured usage would be respected, while the natural instincts of a father would also be satisfied.[122]

Clearly, McLennan, followed here by Frazer, fell into the same trap as F. W. König did when writing about Elamite incestuous marriage and, I fear, with as little success. But at least it puts König in good company, intellectually speaking.

In conclusion, I would reiterate that Herodotus and most of his readers might have been surprised by Lewis Henry Morgan's distinction between classificatory and descriptive kinship terminology, as discussed several times above. As Morgan wrote in *Ancient Society*, "consanguinei are never described, but are classified into categories, irrespective of their nearness or remoteness in degree to *Ego*; and the same term of relationship is applied to all the persons in the same category. Thus . . . my own sisters, and the daughters of my mother's sisters are all alike my sisters."[123] The thrust here should be obvious, particularly since Herodotus specified that Cambyses's first wife was a "full sister." The possibility must at least be entertained that all other "sisters" were potentially classificatory sisters—that is, what we would call cousins. If that is the case, then the charge of brother-sister incest in Cambyses's case may be false, and the question is less Why incest? than What kind of cousin marriage might have been involved, parallel or cross?

122. Frazer 1935, 523–25. Frazer was referring to McLennan 1865.
123. Morgan 1877, 394.

5

Some Aspects of Feudalism in Ancient Iran

When we come to late antiquity there exists a large body of excellent studies on kinship terminology, close-kin or incestuous marriage (Pahlavi *xwēdōdah/ xwēdōdad*), the great aristocratic families, and social organization by a distinguished group of scholars including Arthur Christensen,[1] Touraj Daryaee,[2] Paul Frandsen,[3] Saghi Gazerani,[4] Bodil Hjerrild,[5] Heinrich Hübschmann,[6] Maria Macuch,[7] Katarzyna Maksymiuk,[8] Anahit Perikhanian,[9] Parvaneh Pourshariati,[10] Darab Dastur Peshotan Sanjana,[11] Prods Oktor Skjærvø,[12] Yuhan Sohrab-Dinshaw Vevaina,[13] Edward William West,[14] and Józef Wolski.[15] Rather than reviewing material already fully explicated by these scholars, I have chosen to revisit a topic that has been connected with the Achaemenids, Arsacids, and, particularly, the Sasanians since the nineteenth century—namely, the concept of feudalism in ancient Iran.

1. Christensen 1936, 311–30.
2. Daryaee 2013.
3. Frandsen 2009.
4. Gazerani 2016.
5. Hjerrild 2003, 2006.
6. Hübschmann 1889.
7. Macuch 1991, 2007, 2010, 2014, 2017.
8. Maksymiuk 2015.
9. Perikhanian 1983.
10. Pourshariati 2008, 2017.
11. Sanjana 1888.
12. Skjærvø 2013.
13. Vevaina 2018.
14. West 1882.
15. Wolski 1967, 1989.

FEUDAL TRAITS IN ANCIENT IRAN

Few specialists in medieval European feudalism have probably spent a great deal of time considering the historical debates about feudalism in pre-Islamic Iran. Yet this is a topic of considerable scholarly antiquity in Iranian studies. Nineteenth-century scholars, for example, who relied principally on the data provided by Herodotus and Xenophon, did not hesitate to deem the Achaemenid socioeconomic system feudal. When the Belgian universal historian François Laurent wrote in 1861 that nothing characterized the Persian monarchy so much as its dependent satrapies, he went on to assert that this was feudalism minus the hierarchical principle of organization that defined feudal régimes in Europe.[16] Similarly, in 1882, the French Semitist and historian of religion Ernest Renan claimed that the entire Persian Empire was one vast feudality.[17]

One of the first scholars to offer a broader sketch of what he understood by Iranian feudalism was the Danish Iranologist Arthur Christensen (fig. 12). In 1907, he argued that the origins of feudalism in Persia were to be found in the seven "clans privilégiés," one of which was the Achaemenids.[18] Below these, in rank, were a series of vassals,[19] some of whom had been given land as hereditary fiefs by the great king, although their relationship to the satraps was unclear. Nevertheless, Christensen believed that feudalism remained undeveloped in the Achaemenid era, in part because the Achaemenid kings had a standing army—relieving them of the necessity of relying on levies raised by their vassals—as well as a centralized system of administration.[20]

In the Achaemenid case, much depends on the interpretation of OP *bandaka* in the Bisotun inscription. König considered the *bandaka* to be literally the "bound," in the sense that they were bound to the throne of Darius through vassalage.[21] *Bandaka* was translated as "servicemen or vassals" and "bound ones" by Geo

16. Laurent 1861, 485. Cf. Held 1863, 334n280.

17. Renan 1882, 4.

18. Christensen 1907, 6. Already in 1879, however, Nöldeke (1879, 437) had stressed that the notion of seven clans or "houses" was simply a convention, albeit one attested in the Arsacid and Sasanian periods as well. Cf. Xenophon's account of the trial of Orontas "before the seven 'best' Persians of Cyrus's [the Younger] entourage." See the discussion in Tuplin 2010, 51–52, 59n5. Marquart (1895, 635) noted that, according to Tabari, Kai Wištāsp installed seven hereditary feudal lords, making each one the ruler of a province. The number seven here is suspect, at best. For a discussion of groups of seven "witches, other demons and monsters, gods," in Sumerian and Akkadian literature and religion, see Konstantopoulos (2015, 15). One is also reminded here of the seven journeys across seven mountains in the Sumerian poem *Enmerkar and the Lord of Aratta* (Vanstiphout 1983, 40–41) or the seven "brother warriors" in *Gilgamesh and Huwawa* (Civil 2003). Obviously, the number seven in these cases has a strong folkloric flavor.

19. Christensen 1907, 6–7. Cf. Christensen 1936, 14.

20. Christensen 1907, 7.

21. König 1938, 57n4.

FIGURE 12. Arthur Christensen *(left foreground)* and Henri Massé at the Ferdowsi millennial celebration in 1934. Photograph by the British poet and dramatist John Drinkwater. © 2020 The Nelson Collection of Qajar Photography; used with permission of John Ferreira.

FIGURE 13. Jacques de Morgan (1857–1924). Wikimedia Commons (public domain).

Widengren;[22] "subordinate/vassal" by Iris Colditz;[23] and "bondsman" by Wilhelm Eilers.[24] As Ernst Badian noted, "OP *bandaka*, one 'bound' to a superior, especially the King . . . is the term that Darius I uses throughout the Bisutun inscription to designate his senior army officers, most strikingly even a member of the 'six families' that had assisted in his *coup d'état* and hence held the highest position in the Persian aristocracy."[25] Widengren emphasized that, when looking at comparable Neo-Babylonian terms, the simple translation "servant" or "slave" would be incorrect because it failed to indicate the semantic field of the term with its connotations of a military subordinate. This view is echoed by Wouter Henkelman, who stressed that "in Bīsotūn [Elamite] *libar-uri* (sg., equivalent of OPers *mantetā bandaka*) is used for Darius' generals and seems to denote 'my follower,' 'my vassal' rather than 'my servant.'"[26] Darius also called Dādarši, satrap of Bactria, and Vivāna, satrap of Arachosia, *manā bandaka*.[27]

For Jacques de Morgan (fig. 13), "the great vassals or companions of the supreme chief" in the Achaemenid Empire consisted of a class of nobility to which

22. Widengren 1969, 13–14.
23. Colditz 2000, 110.
24. Eilers 1988.
25. Badian 2000, 250.
26. Henkelman 2003, 105.
27. Schmitt 1991, 63 [DB III 13] and 65 [DB III 56].

the younger branches of the royal family and the principal chiefs of tribes which had taken part in the conquest belonged. The seigniors themselves in their provincial governments surrounded themselves with their principal subordinates, descendants of those who had served under their ancestors at the time of the invasion. After the conquest each of the chief vassals was granted or received a territory proportionate to the importance of his tribe, and the same was done for each of the clans, then for the families. Thus a kind of complete hierarchy was established from the owner of a village or a group of tents up to the supreme master.[28]

This was a characterization that, while flatly contradicting Laurent's perception of a lack of hierarchy, seems to owe just a bit too much inspiration to land tenure in late Qajar Iran as witnessed firsthand by Morgan.[29]

In a similar vein, the German ancient historian Hermann Bengtson wrote that if one wished to identify the essence of the Persian Empire, it was as a kind of feudal state, even though it changed through time. The feudal-vassal system, organized down to the smallest unit, he suggested, served mainly to guarantee military service. The sovereignty of certain families, from which the highest ranking bureaucrats were drawn, was also typical of Achaemenid feudalism, he wrote. Individual satrapies often remained in the hands of the same family for multiple generations,[30] giving rise in some cases to satrapal revolts since the satraps assumed the role of great feudal lords.[31] For Ernst Herzfeld, however, the origin of feudalism in Iran, a millennium before it appeared in Europe, according to his chronology, lay in the notion that Ahura Mazda distributed to rich and poor alike their share of land and wealth. In this sense, then, Darius was the feudal "Liege Lord," comparable to the much later "shadow of God."[32]

The provision of a fixed number of days of mounted military service in return for a fief or *feudum* has often been cited as a foundational principle of vassalage.[33] The granting of land in return for service was not, of course, an invention of the European Middle Ages. The same phenomenon is attested in the ancient Near East in many different settings—for example, in Mesopotamia[34] and Egypt.[35] Geo Widengren noted in 1956 that the provision of a fixed number of cavalrymen, archers, and chariot drivers in return for land could be found in the second millennium BC

28. De Morgan 1914: 580.

29. Christensen (1934) noted, in his review of Hüsing 1933 on feudalism, that analogies to more recent Persian and Turkish social systems, separated by thousands of years from the Achaemenid example, were unreliable.

30. Cf. König 1924 and 1926b on the Persian noble families. Examples of "dynastically occupied satrapies" included Phrygia, where the Pharnakids ruled; Caria, under the Hecatomnids; and Cappadocia, where the family of Anaphas was in power. See Klinkott 2005, 47.

31. Bengtson 1937, 115.

32. Herzfeld 1938a, 153.

33. See, e.g., Prestwich 2003, 301; Reynolds 2017, 5.

34. For one relatively recent discussion, see Brinkman 2006.

35. See, e.g., Winckler 1901b, 47, 79, 117, 160; Koschaker 1935b, 18–19; Bengtson 1937, 115–16; Brundage 1956; Widengren 1969, 8–12; Lafont 1998; and Jansen-Winkeln 1999.

at Nuzi.[36] In fact, Codex Hammurabi §27 stipulated that so-called *ilku*-land—that is, land for service—that had been assigned to a soldier or, interestingly, a fisherman, who had subsequently been taken captive, could be reassigned to someone else, but if the original holder of that land returned, it would be restored to him, along with his service obligation.[37] In her exhaustive review of feudalism in the ancient Near East, Sophie Démare-Lafont cited only the Babylonian evidence when dealing with the Achaemenid period, where, indeed, numerous attestations of land-for-service or its alternative, silver-for-service, are attested.[38] Widengren, however, also noted that, judging by the testimony of Xenophon, the character of these fiefs seems to have changed by the late Achaemenid period and become instruments of financial speculation in the hands of craftsmen and workers who no longer supplied manpower for the military.[39] Apart from the fact that Xenophon's testimony cannot always be taken at face value,[40] the evidence cited by Widengren was, again, almost exclusively from the Achaemenid satrapy of Babylonia. More recent studies of Achaemenid feudalism have stressed the importance of vassalage and the pledge of loyalty or homage through *proskynesis* rather than fiefs,[41] but Christopher Tuplin, to name just one scholar, has criticized the notion that Achaemenid feudalism emerged in the same way as it did in early medieval Europe, concluding that infantry were generally more important in the Achaemenid military than cavalry and that the Achaemenid socioeconomic context was "radically different" from that of Europe over a millennium later.[42]

In fact, since the early nineteenth century, many scholars have expressed the view that the most compelling evidence of feudal relations in ancient Iran dates not to the Achaemenid but to the Arsacid and Sasanian periods. The renowned professor of Semitic languages at the Collège de France Étienne-Marc Quatremère (1782–1857), for example, considered the petty kings of Armenia, Media, Elymais, Adiabene, Bactria, and Gordyene all vassals of the Arsacid king who were obliged to march when he required them and to accompany him into battle, fighting beneath the Arsacid banner, even if, in some cases, their own power surpassed that of their sovereign.[43] Similarly, in the posthumously published fragments of his

---

36. Widengren 1956, 108.

37. Roth 1995, 86; Badamchi 2019, 150.

38. Lafont 1998, 620–28. On feudal aspects of Achaemenid Babylonia, see also Cardascia 1983; Stolper 1985, 25n96, 27–28, 54, 59, 69, 105, 150.

39. Widengren 1956, 109. The literature on these fiefs is extensive. As van der Spek (1985, 255), paraphrasing Dandamaev, wrote, "the fief system declined because the fiefs, in the course of time, were divided by inheritance, so that they became too small to support a soldier. . . . It seems that the obligation to serve in the army could be bought off with silver." Cf. Dandamaev 1992, 16.

40. See, e.g., the discussion of the tendentious nature of Xenophon's *Cyropaedia*, which was written, in the opinion of Christesen (2006), to argue for military reform in Sparta, not as a biography of Cyrus the Great.

41. See, e.g., Petit 2004. Cf. also Petit (1990, 248–51) for a discussion of feudality and vassalage.

42. Tuplin 2010, 58.

43. Quatremère 1840, 341.

history of the Arsacids, Jean-Antoine Saint-Martin (1791–1832) reminded readers that, according to Strabo, Iran was governed by vassal kings of the Arsacid great king and that one such vassal within the Arsacid feudal structure in the early third century was none other than Ardašīr, founder of the Sasanian empire.[44] As Iris Colditz observed, although Widengren emphasized the comparability of Iranian and European social institutions, and consequently posited a developed form of feudalism in Iran, this applied only to the Arsacid period. Hans Heinrich Schaeder, however, proposed that not until the Sasanian period did a fully feudal society emerge.[45] In his 1943 study of Sasanian art, Kurt Erdmann suggested that forms of "knighthood" were developed in Iran long before they were in the West, which, he believed, owed much to Eastern influences later transmitted to Europe by returning crusaders.[46] Even so, Touraj Daryaee has expressed some reserve, noting that, while "the characteristics of land tenure or 'feudal' makeup in the Near East and in particular in Iran have similarities with European feudalism . . . there are major differences as well."[47] But rather than throwing the baby out with the bath water, Josef Wiesehöfer has suggested that "although former studies on Sasanian 'feudalism' very often drew unjustified and wrong parallels between Sasanian Iran and the medieval European monarchies the theoretical parameters of studies on late medieval and early modern courts proved to be quite useful for cutting a swathe through the source material on the Sasanian court and on power and 'state-building' in Sasanian Iran."[48]

MARKERS OF NOBILITY

One feature of feudal society implied by the system of vassalage is the existence of a class composed of families whose wealth and land, as well as loyalty to a sovereign or his/her heirs, persisted through time—in other words, a form of hereditary nobility. Arthur Christensen conceived of ancient Iranian society, in the Avestan tradition, as reflected in the Gāthās, as four-tiered, consisting of the house (*nmana-*), village (*vis-*), tribe (*zantu-*) and province (*dahyu-*). In his opinion, during the Achaemenid period, the king occupied the position of chief of the land, while the positions formerly held by tribal chiefs were now the domain of satraps. Below them came the clan chiefs (*visbadh*) and heads of families or households (*mānbadh*),[49] which were identified eponymously, as Antoine Meillet emphasized, by their heads' names.[50] In the Arsacid and Sasanian periods,

---

44. Saint-Martin 1850, 50–51, 174.
45. Colditz 2000, 111n18.
46. Erdmann 1969, 73.
47. Daryaee 2010, 401–2. Toponyms containing *diz-*, however, point to the existence of castles or fortifications (e.g., *diz-pul*, mod. Dizfūl). Cf. Hübschmann 1897, 19.
48. Wiesehöfer 2010, 143.
49. Christensen 1936, 13, 15.
50. Meillet 1925, 23.

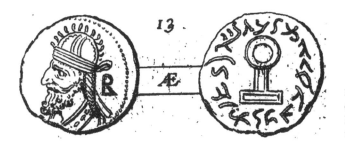

FIGURE 14. A drachm of Vologases III (after Pellérin 1767, Pl. 1.13).

however, we encounter both these magnates, and the names of great families, like the Suren, Karin, and Mehran, that dominated Iranian society for centuries.[51]

In discussing the significance of kinship ties in medieval Europe, which he believed had been over-estimated, David Herlihy found that the vast majority of charters recording land transactions from the eighth century onward rarely reflected "the permission or agreement of kinsmen"; moreover, "whatever the strength of family sentiment or the moral weight of the obligation to demand vengeance, the extended kinship group had little visible importance as an economic administrator, at least in regard to the management of land." In fact, family names were rare until the late tenth century and remained so for the next few centuries. "Apart from the high aristocracy, there seems little consciousness of membership in an identifiable kinship group, and little memory of a common ancestry."[52] In Sasanian Iran, however, we are certainly justified in considering families like Suren, Karin, and Mehran exceptional, powerful kinship units, evidence of which Herlihy only saw much later in Europe.

In Western scholarship, examples of signs used by Parthian and Sasanian noble houses have been known since the earliest drawings of Arsacid and Sasanian coins and reliefs began appearing in publications by Enlightenment scholars,[53] even if these often went unremarked upon. Examples include those published in the *Supplement* to Joseph Pellerin's *Recueils des médailles*, from 1767 (fig. 14), and Carsten Niebuhr's report on his 1765 visit to Fars, published in 1778, in which drawings of the Nāqš-e Rostām I and VI rock reliefs[54] show such devices on the headgear of two of the attendants (fig. 15).

By the early nineteenth century, greater attention was being paid to these devices. In the 1822 account of his travels, Sir Robert Ker Porter commented on the very same heraldic devices on the rock reliefs at Nāqš-e Rostām that Niebuhr

51. These have been discussed extensively in the Iranological literature. For the names Suren and Karin, see, e.g., Schmitt (1983); and Pourshariati (2017). The Mehran family boasted the famous general Warahrān Čobin; see, e.g., Maksymiuk (2015, 191; and Syvänne and Maksymiuk (2018, 28, 30).

52. Herlihy 1970, 67–68.

53. See, e.g., Pellerin 1767; Niebuhr 1778.

54. These are modern numberings and follow those used in Vanden Berghe 1983.

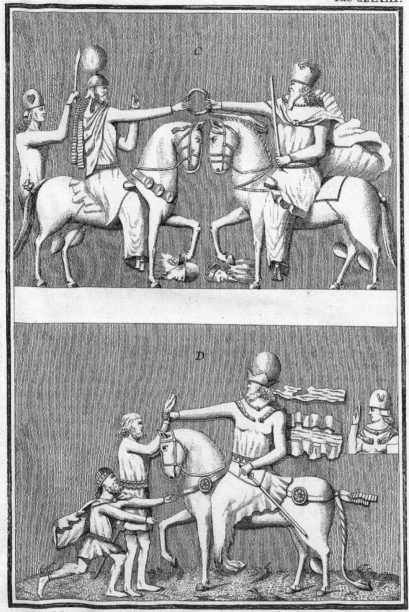

Tab XXXIII.

Abbildung der Figuren zu Nakschi Ruſtam.

FIGURE 15. Carsten Niebuhr's illustrations of Naqš-e Rostām I (upper) and VI (lower) (after Niebuhr 1778, 2: table 33).

FIGURE 16. Naqš-e Rostām I, by Sir Robert Ker Porter (after Ker Porter 1821, 1: between 548 and 549).

had illustrated half a century earlier. Nāqš-e Rostām I (fig. 16), depicting the investiture of Ardašīr, includes "a beardless youth, wearing a high round-topped cap, on which is some distinguishing mark," which, Ker Porter thought, seemed "to place him in the same rank with the figure half covered with the scroll in the bas-relief of Shapoor." On Nāqš-e Rostām VI (fig. 17), showing Šābuhr I's triumph, the bust of Kerdir appears wearing "a round-topped cap . . . with a sort of badge on its side, like part of a flower." Finally, on Nāqš-e Rostām II (fig. 18), which shows Warahrān II with members of his family and other dignitaries, the headgear worn includes some with "a crescent, with a small circle over it," or "the crescent only," or "again a mark on it not unlike that on the fanning attendant" depicted on another relief there.[55] Generally, Ker Porter suggested, "the different flat marks"[56] seen on the headgear of these reliefs "are likely to have been badges of the respective rank or function of the wearer."[57]

---

55. Ker Porter 1821, 541, 551, 559.
56. By this he meant they were carved in low relief.
57. Ker Porter 1821, 561.

FIGURE 17. Naqš-e Rostām VI, by Sir Robert Ker Porter (after Ker Porter 1821, 1: between 540 and 541).

FIGURE 18. Naqš-e Rostām II, by Sir Robert Ker Porter (after Ker Porter 1821, 1: between 556 and 557).

These marks quickly found their way into studies such as Adalbert de Beaumont's 1853 monograph on the origins of European heraldry.[58] Even if Richard N. Frye's comparison between pre-Islamic camel brands and European coats of arms seems somewhat stretched,[59] it is undeniable that the use of signs to mark property and to identify families, lineages, clans, dynasties, and high-ranking individuals is historically widespread in both space and time.[60] There exists a great variety of what have been called variously "heraldic devices,"[61] "*tamgas*,"[62] "émblems,"[63] or, to use their ancient, Middle Persian name, "*nīšān*,"[64] and it has often been argued that these were the equivalent of later European familial *Wappenzeichen*,[65] "wappenartigen Zeichen,"[66] or *blasons*.[67] Here, following Robert Göbl, I will refer to these as *tamgas*, a word signifying "seal" in Old Turkic and "printing plate" in Mongolian.[68] It has been suggested, though, that these are secondary meanings, the primary being "a property-mark"[69] used by a family or clan on livestock, where it appears as

---

58. Beaumont 1853, 51–53, 109–10.

59. Frye 1987, 17. He was, of course, not the first to draw attention to camel brands. See, e.g., Gennep 1902; and Artin Pacha 1902, 182–220, 235, 239–40, 242, with a bibliography.

60. The literature on this subject is voluminous. See, e.g., Beaumont 1853; Homeyer 1870; Andree 1889, 74–85; Artin Pacha 1902; Meyermann 1904; and Gennep 1905.

61. Bivar 1959; Bivar 1970, 399.

62. Nickel 1973; Göbl 1976, 83; Yatsenko 2010a, 2010b; Manassero 2013.

63. Bromberg 1990, 1; Shokoohy 1994.

64. Göbl 1976, 83.

65. Erdmann 1969, 55, 73; Göbl 1976, 83.

66. Herzfeld 1926, 254.

67. Ghirshman 1946, 11. Cf. Ghirshman 1956, 73–74.

68. Erdal 1991, 378. For a possible Alanic etymology, see Manassero (2013, 60). Discussing the Kalmucks, Pallas (1776, 65) noted the use of a signet ring with the personal *tamga* in signing an oath. On the Mongols, Pallas (1776, 189) noted that the Khan signified his approbation of the decisions of his council with his signature or the impression of his seal (*tamga*) in red or black ink.

69. Laufer 1917, 117. Doerfer (2011) noted that "the *tamḡā* 'mark of ownership' originally identified the communal property of a kinship group or tribe. It occurred chiefly as a cattle brand but also on such objects as vases; it was also scratched on stones bearing inscriptions. It contrasted with the *ṭoḡrā* (Middle Turkish *tuḡraḡ*), an individual's symbol (later often represented by a device of reign, valid for the respective ruler). After the Turks acquired a chancellery practice, *tamḡā* came to mean 'the stamping of a document as the ruler's property,' hence 'originating from the ruler,' hence 'seal.'" Discussing the Kirghiz-Kaisak, Jochelson (1928, 129–30) noted:

> The subclan crest or *tamga* may be regarded as its symbol. The crest is used as a property mark and is branded on the left side of the animal, i.e., the side from which the rider mounts, or cut on various belongings, as well as on the graves of deceased members of the clan. The *tamga*, represented by geometric designs, may correspond to a totem. Some of the Kirghiz of the Middle Horde have *tamgas* representing a "bird's rib" *(urdas bii)*, a comb *(tarak)*, and a forked stick *(salak)*. The antiquity of these symbols can be judged from the fact that they may be seen on the old Nestorian monuments and on the monument to Khan Kul-Jegi in the valley of the Orkhon, on which the inscriptions are in old Turkic characters, dating from 732 A.D.

Göbl (1971, 100) isolated symbols and *tamgas* as one iconographic category on Sasanian stamp seals. These he described as that which one often called "heraldic devices," and marks of authority.

a brand, and on other objects.[70] Such signs appear as status markers[71] on, for example, the headgear of certain individuals depicted on the Sasanian reliefs described above, only when and if a particular family, lineage, or clan assumed a leading role socially and politically.[72] Thus, this was a further development from the original function and meaning of the *tamga*.[73] In 1971, Göbl argued that despite the fact that the term *tamga* was only attested long after the Sasanian period, it was nevertheless the best descriptor available for those heraldic devices that already appeared on the helmets and headgear of early Sasanian elites and that, like heraldic coats of arms, served as unique, unambiguous identifiers of individuals.[74]

The literature on *tamgas* has a long history. In Rašid al-Dīn's history of the Oghuz, we find a reference to the fact that Oghuz told his son Kün-Ḥān that each of the twenty-four sections of the Oghuz should have its individual sign and *tamga* in order that their rank, function, and title might be recognized and so as to avoid internal strife.[75] Similarly, according to the so-called political and military institutes of Temur, the world conqueror gave a dozen of his elite troops each a distinctive mark or *tamga*.[76] In 1928, Ernst Herzfeld suggested that *tamgas* were abstractions—abbreviated and simplified versions of originally figural depictions derived from the property ownership marks of previously nomadic peoples—that had evolved into clan or lineage markers, variants of which might be used by individuals or families. In this sense, he believed, they truly did mirror European heraldic devices. Whereas distinctive crowns or headgear were used to identify kings and gods, *tamgas* ("blasons") were used to identify persons.[77] *Tamgas* have also been interpreted as abbreviated titles or designations of rank.[78]

TAMGAS ON SASANIAN RELIEFS

Already visible on the drawings of the Nāqš-e Rostām reliefs published by Niebuhr and Ker Porter in the late eighteenth and early nineteenth centuries, the entire corpus of *tamgas* depicted on Sasanian rock reliefs was collected more than fifty years

---

70. As Göbl (1967, 203) noted, a *tamga* was a personal property mark, belonging to a family or clan. It was, first and foremost, a brand used to distinguish the horses, cattle, and sheep of one household from another.

71. Jänichen 1956.

72. As Gennep (1905, 106) noted, the transformation of a property mark into an armorial one only occurred where there was a social differentiation between nobles and commoners—for example, among the Kirgiz.

73. Göbl 1967, 204.

74. Göbl 1971, 109–10.

75. Jahn 1969, 45. Cf. Anonymous 1860, 112; and Nickel 1973, fig. 14.

76. Davy 1781, 309; Langlès 1787, 151; Csiky 2006, 462.

77. Herzfeld 1928, 130. Cf. Steindorff in Horn and Steindorff 1891, 1.

78. Yatsenko 2010a, 113.

FIGURE 19. Fīrūzābād I, by Eugène Flandin, 1851–54. Etching by Auguste Alexandre Guillaumot. New York Public Library Digital Collections. http://digitalcollections.nypl.org /items/510d47e2-8f8c-a3d9-e040-e00a18064a99.

ago by Erich F. Schmidt.[79] Those seen on Ardašīr I's battle relief at Fīrūzābād, where three pairs of combatants appear, have attracted particular attention (fig. 19).[80] The lead combatant is Ardašīr, shown unhorsing the last Arsacid king, Ardavān or Artabanus. Herzfeld was particularly struck by the *tamga* covering Ardašīr's horse,[81] which Roman Ghirshman thought represented the ring and ribbons, or crown and diadem, given by Ahuramazdā to the king in investiture scenes.[82]

The crown and diadem[83] shown in investiture scenes are not confined to the reliefs of Ardašīr, however, as those commemorating the investitures of Narseh, Šābuhr II, and Xosrow II clearly show. For Richard N. Frye, the *tamga*'s placement on the horse ridden by Xosrow II in the great grotto at Tāq-e Bostān IV (fig. 20) was also telling. As he noted, "Since a *tamgha* was used by Turks and Mongols in branding horses, it is perhaps not inappropriate that the first of the Sasanian signs [first by virtue of its use by Ardašīr, founder of the Sasanian empire] is also found on the flank of a horse on a Sasanian relief at Taq-i Bostān."[84] In fact, in 1938, Herzfeld had suggested that the presence of Ardašīr's "Diadem-Zeichen" on the horse identified since the time of Hamd-Allah Mostawfi (c. 1281–1344) as Shabdīz, "black as night,"[85] Xosrow's famous steed, could imply that Ardašīr, the founder of the Sasanian Empire, had also established a royal stud, from which Xosrow's horse

79. See Schmidt 1970, table 5.
80. Hinz 1969, 115. For excellent illustrations and discussion of the entire relief program, see also Gall 1990.
81. Herzfeld 1926, 254.
82. Ghirshman 1946, 9.
83. Kaim 2009, 405.
84. Frye 1963, 176.
85. Mostawfi called Taq-e Bostan the "Stall of Shabdīz." See the discussion in d'Anville (1761, 162); and Silvestre de Sacy (1793, 235–36). Cf. Potts 2018b, 587; Potts 2022c, 251; Thomas 1873a, 84; Jackson 1920, 12.

FIGURE 20. Tāq-e Bostān IV, by Eugène Flandin, 1851–54. Etching by Auguste Alexandre Guillaumot. New York Public Library Digital Collections. http://digitalcollections.nypl.org /items/510d47e2-8f61-a3d9-e040-e00a18064a99.

FIGURE 21.
Vologases IV Æ
tetrachalkon from
Edessa. BMC 96,
Sellwood 84.134.
Used with permis-
sion of wildwinds
.com, ex cngcoins
.com, Auction 88,
Sept. 2011.

came several centuries later, bearing what had originally been Ardašīr's brand.[86] If this device was, in fact, derived from the crown and diadem used in investi-ture ceremonies, then its appearance at Firūzabād may reflect Ardašīr's desire to underscore his legitimacy when appearing in battle, even though he was the chal-lenger and not, at that point, the legitimate king.

Roman Ghirshman, who called the device on Ardavān's horse "the emblem of the Parthian king, a ring placed upon a support," also noted that it was attested on the coinage of the Arsacid kings Vologases III[87] and IV (fig. 21), as Herzfeld had

86. Herzfeld (1938b, 108) suggested that Ardašīr's *tamga* became almost a family sign, used by his son Šābuhr I, alongside his own; both were used by his grandson Narseh, as if he wanted to declare his legitimate right to the throne, and later by Warahrān (III) and Šābuhr II. Then, after a long gap, it reappeared on Xosrow's mount.

87. Ghirshman 1946, 8–9n3, referring to Morgan, *Numismatique orientale*, p. 168, fig. 180C.

already observed.[88] It is also emblazoned on Ardavān's headgear at Nāqš-e Rostām. In a slim monograph heavily criticized by Robert Göbl for its superficiality, the German archivist Hans Jänichen noted that the same device appeared on the coinage of Phraates IV and Vologases I, as well as Vologases III,[89] and it has been chosen by Fabrizio Sinisi as the logo for the *Sylloge Nummorum Parthicorum*.[90]

A straightforward interpretation of these co-occurrences would suggest a familial relationship between all of these rulers, including Ardavān, but this would be incorrect since we know, for example, that Phraates IV belonged to the Sinatrucid line—that is, the descendants of Sinatruces who came to power around 78 BC and were probably descendants of Mithradates I. The "House of Vologases I or Vologasids," however, represented a rival line, descended from Artabanus II and his brother Vonones, which perhaps originated with Mithradates II.[91] Given the animosity between these two extended families, one would not expect them to have shared the same *tamga*. As for the episodic, discontinuous appearance of the *tamga* on Arsacid coinage, Sinisi has suggested, following the late David Sellwood, that this reflected political expediency. These scholars have argued that the decision to illustrate the *tamga* on coinage was "associated with phases of political unrest, when Vologases allegedly decided to distinguish his issues from the coins struck by the rebels challenging his authority."[92]

Turning again to the Firūzabād relief: Ardašīr's son, the crown prince Šābuhr, is shown riding a horse covered with a different *tamga* than that of his father, one that adorns his quiver as well. Herzfeld referred to Šābuhr's *tamga* as the Arsacid *ankh*-sign embellished with a crescent moon,[93] while Ghirshman called it a crescent mounted on a ring support.[94] In his 1963 review of Göbl's publication of the Sasanian coins in the royal numismatic collection in The Hague, Frye discussed the *tamgas* of both Ardašīr and Šābuhr: "Inasmuch as the *tamgha* of Ardavān . . . is similar to that of Šāpūr, minus the crescent on the circle, we may suggest that the sign of Šāpūr is that of a noble Arsacid family, close to that of Ardavān, from whom Šāpūr's mother came."[95] Frye is alluding here to the different traditions surrounding the filiation of Ardašīr's wife, identified variously as Ardavān's daughter (by Tabārī), a cousin (according to the anonymous *Nihayat ul-'arab*), or as the daughter of an unnamed Arsacid nobleman (thus Dinawārī).[96] In 1985 Frye's hypothesis was repeated by David Sellwood, Philip Whitting, and Richard Williams, who saw

88. Herzfeld 1938b, abb. 4.

89. Jänichen 1956, pl. 26. This had already been observed by Herzfeld 1938b, 108.

90. Fabrizio Sinisi (pers. comm.) confirms that the *tamga* on coins attributed by David Sellwood to Vologases IV appears on coins reassigned to Vologases III in Sinisi (2012, 63n251).

91. See the discussion of these familial/dynastic lineages in Olbrycht (2016).

92. Sinisi 2012, 63.

93. Herzfeld 1938b, 108.

94. Ghirshman 1946, 10n2. Thomas (1873b, 32) called this "the sun and moon in conjunction"; Hinz (1969, 119) considered it a ring on a T-shaped support surmounted by a crescent moon; and Bivar (1970, 399) referred to it as the "cap-device."

95. Frye (1963, 176) is following a suggestion first made in Herzfeld (1938b, 108).

96. See Pourshariati (2008, 45–46) for a discussion of these sources.

two possible explanations for the origin of Šābuhr's *tamga*, which they unhesitatingly called a "dynastic symbol." The first was that it was derived from Ardavān's *tamga*, as Frye had suggested more than two decades earlier. The second was that it had "Gondopharean precedents,"[97] a notion that goes back at least to Herzfeld's 1938 paper on Tāq-e Bostān[98] and that both Saghi Gazerani and Marek Olbrycht have recently revived, suggesting that the *tamga* on Šābuhr's horse and quiver is the same as that used as a "dynastic mintmark on Gondopharid coinage"—that is, the issues of the eastern Indo-Parthian state that ruled in Arachosia, Drangiana, and Sakastan during the last century BC and first century AD.[99] Related to this hypothesis, Olbrycht has further speculated that Farn-Sāsān, the last king of the Gondopharid dynasty, was actually Ardašīr's father. Although he did not make the connection explicitly, Olbrycht implied that the Gondopharid *tamga* and that found on Šābuhr's horse and quiver are testimony to this familial tie. Gazerani, in contrast, following Herzfeld, suggested that the "Gondopharid symbol," as she calls it, was "a symbol of the house of Suren,"[100] the members of which were considered instrumental in bringing Ardašīr to power, according to Olbrycht.

There is a problem with this hypothesis, however, which Herzfeld, Gazerani, and Olbrycht all appear to have glossed over. Simply stated, the Gondopharid *tamga* and the *tamga* of Šābuhr I are not graphically identical. The open circle in the middle of the Gondopharid device is topped not by the crescent seen on Šābuhr's horse and quiver but by two diagonal lines, either meant to be read as individual lines or as a V atop an open circle. Particularly given the lunar associations of crescents, whether in combination with other elements, as seen here, or on their own, and their potential religious significance, I would be very reluctant to ignore the graphic differences between these two signs.[101]

Finally, we come to the third Sasanian nobleman depicted at Firūzabād who wears headgear decorated with a floral symbol, a *tamga* that appears on his horse as well. Ghirshman suggested this figure was the page,[102] who is also shown holding a fly whisk behind Ardašīr at Nāqš-e Rostām.[103]

A *TAMGA* ON THE HEADGEAR OF WARAHRĀN IV

Besides appearing on Sasanian reliefs, *tamgas* are visible on a large number of Sasanian seals and coins, where they are often referred to as "Beizeichen" (symbols).[104]

97. Sellwood, Whitting, and Williams 1985, 34.

98. Herzfeld (1938b, 108) called it the sign of the dynasty of Sūrēn Gundopharr of Sakastān.

99. Olbrycht 2016, 24. For the use of this *tamga* by the Gondopharids, called "the Gondopharid sign," see also Shenkar (2017, 176).

100. Gazerani 2016, 22.

101. For a very different interpretation of this device, see Soudavar (2009, 427–28).

102. Herzfeld (1926, 254) called him the *Knappe*, or squire, of Ardašīr.

103. Ghirshman 1946, 11. Sarre and Herzfeld (1910, 69) wrote that the sign on the headgear was probably an indicator of rank.

104. See, e.g., Alram and Gyselen (2003); and Schindel (2004).

One particularly fine object, a large convex bezel made of amethyst, shows the bust of a Sasanian nobleman wearing a *kolāh*, the typical royal headgear,[105] with a *tamga* on it. The accompanying Pahlavi inscription identifies the individual as the prince "Warahrān [IV, r. 388–99] Kirmānšāh ['king,' i.e., governor, of Kerman], son of Šābuhr [III] the Mazdaean, King of Kings of Ērān and An-Ērān, who is of the race of gods."[106] The seal has been known since the eighteenth century and offers an important window on the origins and development of scholarship in this field, as well as the history of collecting and connoisseurship and the repurposing of ancient objects in modern times.

The story begins in 1761, when the German gem engraver Johann Lorenz Natter (1705–63), from Biberach in Swabia,[107] catalogued the gems and seals in the collection of the 4th Duke of Devonshire.[108] The Devonshire collection, kept to this day at Chatsworth (Derbyshire, UK), was begun by the 4th Duke's grandfather William, 2nd Duke of Devonshire, who succeeded to the title in 1707 and amassed a large coin collection. Both the 3rd and 4th dukes added to the collection. In a catalogue dating to 1908, the then Chatsworth librarian and later assistant director of the British School at Rome, Eugénie Sellers Strong (1860–1943), speculated that "the 4th Duke had relied on [Baron Philipp von] Stosch for many of his acquisitions, and Stosch was certainly familiar with the collection, for some of his opinions were quoted by Natter" in his unpublished catalogue of 1761.[109] Baron Philipp von Stosch (1691–1757), who spent much of his life in Florence and Rome,[110] amassed what was almost certainly the largest collection of engraved gems and

---

105. For a discussion of this headgear, see Gyselen (1989, 152).

106. Ouseley 1801, 17–18. This was immediately confirmed by Silvestre de Sacy (1801, 358). Cf. Gyselen 1989, 160, no. Z2 and pl. 2.22. On the basis of the "exquisite naturalism of the portrayal and the appearance of the eye and beard," Harper (1974, 69; cf. Harper 1978, 142) suggested that this seal depicts Warahrān I, not Warahrān IV. Responding to this, Bivar (1985, 34) wrote that if this was correct, then Warahrān I "too, prior to his imperial accession, will have held charge of Kirmān province as Kirmānshāh," but this is unlikely. As Shahbazi (2016) stressed, Warahrān I, son of Šābuhr I, was Gēlānšāh—that is, king/governor—of Gilan near the Caspian Sea, according to the Kaʿba-ye Zardošt inscription. Warahrān IV, the son of Šābuhr III, however, was Kirmānšāh. See Klíma 2016. Herzfeld (1924, 1:77–79 and fig. 35; also Herzfeld 1924, 2: fig. 140) discussed the seal briefly, noting its resemblance to another amethyst seal of Warahrān I in St. Petersburg, which differed only in the more rounded form of the *kolāh*. The inscription on the St. Petersburg exemplar reads "Warahrān, the great šāh." See Zakharov 1933, 270.

107. For his career, see Dalton (1915, xlix, with refs). Among his other clients were Catherine the Great, Christian VI of Denmark, and William IV of Orange. According to Mariette (1750, 144), Natter went from Rome to England and then to Iran, attracted by "Thamas-Kouli-Kan"—that is, Nader Shah. This was contradicted by Natter himself, who wrote, "From *Italy* I came to *England*; and went from hence with Mr. Mark Tuscher to *Denmark*, *Sweden* and *Petersburgh*. But never was at the Court of *Thomas Kouli-Kan*, where Mr. Mariette has left me to seek my Fortune." See Natter 1754, xxx.

108. Scarisbrick (1986, 252n27) cited Natter's *Catalogue des pierres gravées de la fameuse collection de Monseigneur le Duc de Devonshire*, of 1761, p. 32, no. 27, where it was called a "very singular engraving." The manuscript of Natter's catalogue is held at Chatsworth.

109. Scarisbrick 1986, 241.

110. For the history of his collection, see, for example, Hansson (2014) and Pietrzak (2018).

FIGURE 22. The Warahrān IV gem cast
(after Tassie and Raspe 1791, 2: no. 673).

FIGURE 23. The Warahrān IV gem cast.
Collection of the author; photo by the
author.

impressions—3,444 originals and glass-paste copies and more than twenty-eight thousand impressions—in the world at that time.[111] After von Stosch's death, no less an important figure in the history of archaeology than Johann Joachim Winckelmann (1717–68) catalogued his collection. But von Stosch's adopted nephew and heir, Heinrich Wilhelm Muzell-Stosch (1723–82), who inherited his uncle's estate,

111. Hansson 2014, 21.

was not interested in keeping or expanding the collection and was instead eager to convert the collection into cash.[112] Accordingly, in 1766, he sold the vast majority of von Stosch's engraved gems to Frederick II of Prussia,[113] while most of the twenty-eight-thousand-plus gem impressions or casts were acquired by James Tassie (1735–99) in Edinburgh. The *catalogue raisonnée* of this collection, which Tassie published in 1791, together with Rudolf Erich Raspe, author of *The Surprising Adventures of Baron Munchausen*, includes an engraving of a sulfur cast of the Warahrān IV seal (fig. 22) and gives its provenience as the von Stosch collection.[114] Recently, a cast of this very same gem (fig. 23) was offered for sale.[115]

As for the seal itself, its provenience prior to entering the Devonshire collection is unknown. On the one hand, it may be that the original Sasanian gem was acquired by the 4th Duke of Devonshire from von Stosch's estate after his death in 1757 but before 1761, when Natter catalogued it at Chatsworth,[116] and in this way the gem was not among the roughly three and a half thousand gems that went to Frederick II of Prussia. On the other hand, we know that, so great was von Stosch's eagerness "to have, if not originals, at least a copy of each known ancient gem,"[117] that he may only have owned the impression, later acquired by Tassie, and never possessed the gem itself, in which case it must have entered the Devonshire collection from another, unknown source. Where the Warahrān seal may have originated prior to its arrival in Europe is unclear, although in discussing Parthian and Sasanian seals circulating in the late eighteenth century, Tassie and Raspe observed that they "come generally from Bassora."[118]

In any case, the engraving of the gem published by Tassie and Raspe in 1791 attracted the notice of Sir William Ouseley (1767–1842), and a decade later he addressed himself to "the Pahlavi inscription on a very curious sulphur described in Mr. Tassie's Catalogue of Gems, (No. 673,) as belonging to the Collection of

112. As Hansson (2014, 25) noted, "Muzell-Stosch, who wanted to travel in the Orient and elsewhere, immediately started negotiating the sale of everything with potential buyers."

113. Hansson 2014, 29. The Persian seals in the catalogue do not include the Warahrān seal. See Winckelmann 1760, 28–32; and Schlichtegroll 1798. Hansson (2014, 26n86) claimed that "the Christian and Persian gems went to the Cavaliere Francesco Vittori," but this is based on a misreading of Justi (1871, 24), who wrote only that the collection of Christian gems was sold after the baron's death, without making any reference to the Persian material.

114. Tassie and Raspe 1791, 1:66, no. 673. As Raspe wrote, "*Sulphur of Stosch* implies an impression taken from and preserved in that numerous collection of Sulphurs which the late Baron *Stosch* formed, and which, *post varios casus*, at last has found its way into Mr. *Tassie's* cabinet." See Tassie and Raspe 1791, 1:lxiv.

115. It is unclear whence this cast derives. A complete set of the casts is held in the Victoria & Albert Museum. The photograph of the Warahrān IV seal, made by the Beazley Archive in Oxford, is unfortunately partially in shadow.

116. Talbot 1861, 301–2.

117. Pietrzak 2018, 122.

118. Tassie and Raspe 1791, 1:67. This, of course, was only their point of sale, not their place of origin.

Baron Stosch."[119] Ouseley, however, said nothing about the device shown clearly on Warahrān's headgear, nor did Antoine Isaac Silvestre de Sacy (1758–1838), the eminent French Semitist and Persian scholar, in his review of Ouseley's work, which appeared in the same year.[120] In 1815, the Tassie impression and Ouseley's publication of it were again discussed by Silvestre de Sacy. This time he noted that Warahrān's headgear bore a symbolic device or monogram, but he made no attempt to explain it.[121] Meanwhile, as Natter's catalogue of the Devonshire collection from 1761 was unpublished, unlike the cast of the seal in the Tassie collection, the existence of the gem itself was presumably known only to the duke and whomever he may have shown it to.

This all changed in 1856, however, when the 6th Duke of Devonshire, a bachelor, had it set, along with eighty-seven other ancient gems, by the London jeweler C. F. Hancock in what has become known as the Chatsworth or Devonshire "parure." This elaborate set of jewelry was made to be worn by Countess Granville, the wife of the duke's nephew Earl Granville, at the coronation of Czar Alexander II in Moscow on 7 September 1856, which they attended as representatives of Queen Victoria. The set of seven pieces, incorporating eighty-eight ancient gems, consisted of a comb, bandeau, stomacher, necklace, diadem, coronet, and bracelet. A contemporary description of it lists "a very fine Oriental Amethyst Intaglio" as the seventh stone in Hancock's comb. Five smaller gems were set in a row above three larger ones, the central one being the Warahrān IV seal.[122] As a writer in the *Manchester Guardian* noted on 28 February 1857, "the comb has an elegant form in outline; its chief gem placed in the centre is a large, pure and lustrous oriental amethyst, on which is carved the head of the Persian King of the ancient Sassanian dynasty with the high cap of sovereign, and at the side is an inscription in this oldest known form of Persian. This gem is undoubtedly antique, the line of kings deriving their dynastic name from Sassan, the grandfather of Artaxerxes"[123] (i.e., Ardašīr).

Within a decade, Edward Thomas referred to the gem as "the Duke of Devonshire's well-known amethyst,"[124] and it quickly entered the literature as "the highly-prized amethyst belonging to the Duke of Devonshire,"[125] "the great Devonshire amethyst,"[126] "the celebrated Devonshire Amethyst,"[127] and a "magnificent amethyst

---

119. Ouseley 1801, 17.

120. Silvestre de Sacy 1801, 358.

121. Silvestre de Sacy (1815, 214) noted that the headgear was adorned with a symbol or monogram that he was at a loss to explicate.

122. Hancock 1857, 5. Cf. Scarisbrick 1986, 247.

123. Anonymous 1857.

124. Thomas 1866, 241 and pl. 8 for an engraving of the seal.

125. Thomas 1868a, 349.

126. King 1872, 1:62.

127. Thomas 1873, 10.

FIGURE 24. The Warahrān IV gem (after Thomas 1868a, 350).

intaglio."[128] Nevertheless, when discussing the Devonshire gem, Thomas lamented that he had "vainly sought to obtain a thoroughly satisfactory representation" and was consequently forced to publish a "woodcut," which "gives a very artistic rendering of the general details."[129] This was later superseded by a more accurate engraving by a Mr. Williams, with the initials "AMW" beneath it (fig. 24).[130] This can only have been Alfred Mayhew Williams (baptized 1832),[131] one of the sons of Samuel Williams (1788–1854), the noted "Engraver on Wood."[132]

The very fact that Warahrān's seal is made of amethyst is significant. Prior to the discovery of extensive amethyst mines in Brazil, the stone was extremely rare,[133] and most of the amethyst consumed in the Roman world derived from mines in the Eastern Desert of Egypt.[134] Given its purple color, amethyst was a "favourite stone for ruler portraits," like the fine intaglio of Gallienus in the British Museum.[135] It is also interesting that "a dramatic revival of gem engraving, including the use of large amethysts and sapphires of fine style," occurred in the fourth century during the reign of Constantine.[136] It has been suggested that in the Sasanian world, seals like the Devonshire amethyst, in the form of "large convex bezels," were typical of senior officials and "may have been a royal prerogative."[137] Given the political situation, it is unlikely that amethyst in late fourth-century Iran, when Warahrān IV

128. Westropp 1874, 88–89.

129. Thomas 1868a, 350.

130. Thomas 1873, 10; originally published in Thomas 1868b, 350.

131. Williams and his four siblings were all baptized in 1832. His date of death is unknown. See Brake and Demoor 2009, 678.

132. Anonymous 1854; Lewer 1917; Avery-Quash 2004.

133. Lüle 2011, 1.

134. Meredith 1957; Shaw and Jameson 1993; Harrell et al. 2006; Hirt 2010, 110.

135. Zwierlein-Diehl 2011, 154 and pl. 28.

136. Spier 2011, 193.

137. Gyselen 2007, 19 and note 77.

reigned, was sourced in Egypt. Either India or Sri Lanka, where sources also exist, is a more likely origin.[138]

In discussing the *tamga* on Warahrān IV's headgear in 1868, Thomas mistook the "highly-prized amethyst belonging to the Duke of Devonshire" and the cast, published by Tassie and Raspe in 1791, for two different seals, noting that on the Tassie cast the "Parthian helmet is adorned with the self-same device as is seen on the more valuable gem,"[139] but he made no attempt to identify or characterize it. A decade later, Andreas David Mordtmann (1811–79) characterized the device on Warahrān IV's headgear as a Zoroastrian symbol.[140]

It is tempting to suggest that the device is composed of Middle Persian letters in Warahrān IV's name, perhaps combined with an epithet, but this remains to be worked out. More complex monograms, which differ from the *tamgas* found on Sasanian rock reliefs, are combinations of letters, often in mirror image, upside down, or at an angle, and can actually be read, as Göbl,[141] Menasce,[142] Adhami,[143] and, more recently, Gyselen and Monsef[144] have shown. More than sixty years ago, Hans Jänichen documented seventy-five different monograms on Sasanian stamp seals,[145] and this number would certainly be greater today. These, as Richard N. Frye pointed out, "were usually representations of names, although the principle that all Sasanian monograms on seals represent the name or legend on the rim of the seals is in *many* cases demonstrably false."[146] In fact, in his 1798 treatise on monograms, Johann Christoph Gatterer noted that monograms, whether on coins, flags, walls or tapestries, seals or documents, could be *nominalia, titularia,* or *verbalia* (names, titles, or words) or a mixture thereof.[147] Sasanian monograms may not represent just one such category.

138. For the Indian and Sri Lankan sources, see, e.g., Gourley and Johnson 2016, 29–31.

139. Thomas 1868b, 111.

140. Mordtmann 1876, 199. Gyselen (1989, 165) made no attempt to interpret the *tamga* and simply referred to it as a symmetrically composed monogram.

141. Göbl 1967; 1976, 85–87 and pl. 48.

142. Menasce 1959. Yatsenko (2010a, 123) maintains, however, that "it is very difficult to interpret them as monograms containing name letters (as it was traditionally thought not long ago), for it is practically impossible to find within them any letters from the Pahlavi alphabet. But they are easily 'divided' into two or three elements, each of them being in most cases identical to the signs of other Iranian peoples. . . . I can suggest that in this case they are compound signs made up of the symbol of the father's clan together with the symbols of the families of the mother and the father." It is possible that the so-called anthropomorphic (?) motifs incised on some of the ceramics from Achaemenid Dahan-e Goleman are *tamgas*. See Zehbari, Afarin, and Haji 2015, 226 and esp. fig. 22.47–53.

143. Adhami 2012.

144. Gyselen and Monsef 2012. Very different interpretations have sometimes been suggested, resulting in polemics. See, e.g., Soudavar (2014, 373–74) vs. Gyselen and Monsef (2012).

145. Jänichen 1956, pl. 23.

146. Frye 1970, 266.

147. Gatterer 1798, 119.

MEANINGS AND SIGNIFIERS

Scholars have viewed the significance of monograms and *tamgas* in very different ways over the years. Whereas monograms have often been seen, implicitly or
explicitly, as ciphers for personal names and titles, even a cursory survey of the
literature on monograms in the non-Iranian world shows that multiple interpretations are often possible,[148] and monograms may be intentionally ambiguous.[149]
Tamgas, however, often appear to be nonreferential abstractions, one notable
exception being the *tamga* on the headgear of the priest (*mobed*) Kerdir, which
resembles a pair of scissors or shears.[150] In theory, either device, whether *tamga*
or a monogram, could have functioned like heraldic devices of medieval Europe,
particularly those seen on the horses of Ardavān, Ardašīr, Šābuhr, and the page
at Firūzabād. It is striking, though, that the nearly three dozen surviving Sasanian rock reliefs were commissioned by just nine of the thirty-one rulers attested
between 224 and 651—namely, Ardašīr I, his son Šābuhr I, and great-grandson
Warahrān II, Narseh, Ōhrmazd II, Šābuhr II, Ardašīr II, Šābuhr III, and Xosrow
II. Furthermore, of those nine rulers who left rock reliefs, only two were depicted
with a *tamga* on their headgear or other equipment: Ardašīr I and Šābuhr I. The

148. To cite just one example, nearly a dozen different explanations, all inconclusive, have been
advanced to decipher the so-called TP (tau-rho) monogram on Herod the Great's year 3 coinage.
See Jacobson 2014, table 1.

149. As in the case of Lady Mary Wroth's (1587?-1651?) "many-sided monogram," the letters of
which "give us the first and last initials of four successive generations of Sidneys, beginning with
Wroth's great-grandfather and ending with herself: William Sidney (WS), Henry Sidney (HS), Robert
Sidney (RS), and Mary Sidney Wroth (MSW). These additional secondary significations would not
have eluded Wroth, nor would the fact that the letters can also spell 'Philip,' reflecting her literary
uncle. . . . These interpretations are possible readings rather than necessary or primary ones." See
Braganza 2022, 144.

150. For his much-discussed *tamga*, in the form of scissors or shears, see Eilers (1974 and 1976)
and Skjærvø (2011/2012), where a host of possibilities are entertained, none of them ultimately satisfying. Mackenzie, on the one hand, suggested that Kerdir's *tamga* might have been a pair of shears or
scissors because these symbolized "his family's trade." See Mackenzie 1999, 257. Skjærvø, on the other
hand, suggested that, if Kerdir was a eunuch, as has sometimes been inferred from his beardlessness
(e.g., Hinz 1969, 228; Lerner and Skjærvø 2006, 116; Skjærvø 2007), then "the shears could have been
a badge of honor," although castration by scissors, as opposed to a razor, knife, or red-hot metal rod
(Wilson and Roehrborn 1999, 4324), appears highly improbable. Certainly, Kerdir's *tamga* does not
resemble Roman castration clamps (for which see, e.g., Francis 1926, figs. 1–7). Grenet (2011, 127),
however, argued persuasively that eunuchs could not be Zoroastrian priests, citing *Yašt* 5.92–93 and
17.53, which require "physical integrity," and suggested instead that being clean-shaven was a precaution against polluting the sacred fire by having one's beard catch on fire, a real danger since the recitation of prayers by the priest was performed very close to the flames. This sort of precaution recalls the
amusing story of the British officer Henry Lindsay (Bethune), charged with training ʿAbbas Mirza's
artillery, who could not convince his trainees that it was safer to be clean-shaven than bearded when
working with explosives. "One day, however, the chance explosion of a powder-horn in the hands of a
gunner carried off the better part of the holder's beard, and Lindsay availed himself of the circum-
stance to gain his end." See Goldsmid 1880, 159.

other figures who bear *tamgas* are unidentified Sasanian elites or dignitaries associated with Ardašīr I, Šābuhr I, and Warahrān II, as well as the last Arsacid king
Ardavān IV or V, the priest (*mobed*) Kerdir, and an unidentified opponent of
Ōhrmazd II. None of the Sasanian magnates or officials depicted alongside Šābuhr
I at Dārāb, however, has a *tamga* on his headgear. So, in brief, the selectivity we
see in the distribution of *tamgas* on Sasanian reliefs would not suggest that these
played the same role as the heraldic insignia of European knights did, and their
significance for the characterization of Sasanian society as feudal is thus in need of
qualification. Their episodic and, indeed, inconsistent use in Iranian late antiquity
raises many questions. If they are deemed markers of feudalism, then many more
societies of the first millennia BC and AD will have to be considered candidates
for that designation as well. However important even the selective use of *tamgas*
on the Iranian plateau may have been, it is an undeniable fact that on the steppes,
from Inner Asia to Hungary, *tamgas* were more widespread in space and time than
they ever were in Iran during the Arsacid and Sasanian periods.

AFTERWORD

It is, perhaps, inevitable that a series of five lectures given on diverse aspects of a particular domain, in this case kinship, do not lend themselves to a convenient, all-encompassing conclusion. This study began with the potential spread of diverse ceramic styles via exogamous marriage patterns and has concluded by examining heraldic devices as individual and family markers. Examples of these and other social practices across several millennia have been interrogated using insights from the rich literature of social anthropology and, occasionally, comparative law. Some practices, deemed aberrant or exceptional, have been shown to reflect patterns that are attested all over the world, across space and time. Yet the aim was never to single out a practice, pair it with a similar one from another cultural context, and thereby uncover a hidden relationship, as a nineteenth-century diffusionist might have done. Rather, it was simply to demonstrate that practices like the preferential marriage patterns of Achaemenid royalty or the privileged position of the sister's son in Elamite royal succession have very real analogues in both ancient and modern societies and were not exceptional but can be accounted for through recourse to the anthropological literature.

The point here has been to underscore the fact that the peoples of ancient Iran, in all periods, may be productively considered through the same lens used to view any culture, and the surest means to arriving at a better comprehension of the social practices of the past is to tap the vast body of social anthropological and historical literature that has been growing for more than two centuries. Archaeologists and historians who focus too strictly on material remains, literary production, or religious ideology risk ignoring the salient features of kinship relations in ancient Iran. This is not a call to privilege the views of anthropologists over those who study the tangible, literary, epigraphic, and archaeological records of the past. It is, rather, a challenge to treat the Iranian evidence with the full arsenal of analytical tools at our disposal. Unlike F. W. König, who seemed to exult in his rejection of comparative anthropological data when discussing the sister's son in ancient Elamite, we have no excuse for not recognizing that the answers to many of the questions that fascinate us are there, if we only make an effort to look for them in the right places. Finding those answers requires casting a wide net and that means, by definition, moving out of the confines of one's own specialty. This requires an open mind, curiosity, patience, and perseverance. Scholars of the twenty-first century benefit every day from the use of search engines and the availability of millions upon millions of pages of searchable, digitized scholarly books and articles, making it easier than ever to uncover comparative material that can help illuminate the most intractable historical problems. Our understanding of Iranian antiquity can advance in directions that are today unknowable, and were yesterday almost unthinkable, when barriers between fields are struck down and the horizons of our inquiry are truly opened up. This presents a challenge for those who have an aversion to leaving their comfort zone, but for others, it provides a road map to a far more exciting way of approaching the past than most of our illustrious academic forebears ever could have envisioned. That, after all is said and done, is what makes scholarship worth pursuing.

ABBREVIATIONS

AA	*American Anthropologist*
AAASH	*Acta Antiqua Academiae Scientiarum Hungaricae*
AfO	*Archiv für Orientforschung*
AMI	*Archäologische Mitteilungen aus Iran*
AOASH	*Acta Orientalia Academiae Scientiarum Hungaricae*
AOAT	Alter Orient und Altes Testament
ArOr	*Archiv Orientální*
BAI	*Bulletin of the Asia Institute*
BIFAO	*Bulletin de l'Institut français d'archéologie orientale*
BSO[A]S	*Bulletin of the School of Oriental and African Studies*
CNIP	Carsten Niebuhr Institute Publications
EKI	siglum of Elamite royal inscriptions published in König 1965
GJ	*Geographical Journal*
HANE/M	History of the Ancient Near East / Monographs
HdO	Handbuch der Orientalistik
IJMES	*International Journal of Middle East Studies*
IrAnt	*Iranica Antiqua*
IrSt	*Iranian Studies*
JA	*Journal Asiatique*
JAOS	*Journal of the American Oriental Society*
JCS	*Journal of Cuneiform Studies*
JESHO	*Journal of the Economic and Social History of the Orient*
JRAI	*Journal of the Royal Anthropological Institute of Great Britain and Ireland*
JRAS	*Journal of the Royal Asiatic Society*
MDP	Mémoires de la Délégation en Perse et varia
OLZ	*Orientalistische Literaturzeitung*

PFa	siglum of Persepolis Fortification texts published in Hallock 1978
PIHANS	Publications de l'Institut historique et archéologique néerlandais de Stamboul
RA	*Revue d'Assyriologie et d'archéologie orientale*
RE	*Pauly-Wissowa Realencyclopädie der classischen Altertumswissenschaft*
RlA	*Reallexikon der Assyriologie*
SANER	Studies in Ancient Near Eastern Records
SAOC	Studies in Ancient Oriental Civilization
SOR	Studia Orientalia Romana
StIr	*Studia Iranica*
UAA	siglum of Elamite texts illustrated in Börker-Klähn 1970
WZKM	*Wiener Zeitschrift für die Kunde des Morgenlandes*
ZA	*Zeitschrift für Assyriologie*
ZDMG	*Zeitschrift der deutschen morgenländischen Gesellschaft*

REFERENCES

Anonymous. 1834. "Biographical Sketch of His Late Royal Highness Abbas Mirza, Prince Royal of Persia, Hon. M.R.A.S.,* &c. &c." *JRAS* 1 (2): 322–25.

Anonymous. 1854. "Mr. Samuel Williams." *Gentleman's Magazine and Historical Review* 41:101.

Anonymous. 1857. "The Jewels Worn by the Countess of Granville at the Emperor of Russia's Coronation." *Manchester Guardian*, 28 Feb.

Anonymous. 1860. "Arbeiten der morgenländischen Abtheilung der kaiserlich archäologischen Gesellschaft." *Archiv für wissenschaftliche Kunde von Russland* 19:109–21.

Anonymous. 1873. "The Reigning Family of Persia." *Saint Pauls Magazine* 12 (Jan.–June): 706–17.

Adhami, S. 2003. "Another Installment on Sasanian Sphragistic Monograms." *ZDMG* 153:275–80.

Alizadeh, A. 1988. "Socio-economic Complexity in Southwestern Iran during the Fifth and Fourth Millennia B.C.: The Evidence from Tall-I Bakun A." *Iran* 26:27–34.

———. 2006. *The Origins of State Organizations in Prehistoric Highland Fars, Southern Iran: Excavations at Tall-E Bakun.* Chicago: Oriental Institute of the University of Chicago.

———. 2008. *Chogha Mish II: The Development of a Prehistoric Regional Center in Lowland Susiana, Southwestern Iran. Final Report on the Last Six Seasons of Excavations, 1972–1978.* Vol. 1. Chicago: Oriental Institute of the University of Chicago.

———. 2010. "The Rise of the Highland Elamite State in Southwestern Iran: 'Enclosed' or Enclosing Nomadism?" *Current Anthropology* 51:353–83.

Allen, W. L., and J. B. Richardson. 1971. "The Reconstruction of Kinship from Archaeological Data: The Concepts, the Methods, and the Feasibility." *AA* 36:41–53.

Alram, M., and R. Gyselen. 2003. *Sylloge Nummorum Sasanidarum Paris—Berlin—Wien, Band I. Ardashir I.—Shapur I.* Vienna: Denkschriften der Österreichischen Akademie der Wissenschaften, phil.-hist. Kl. 317.

Alt, K., and W. Vach. 1991. "The Reconstruction of 'Genetic Kinship' in Prehistoric Burial Complexes—Problems and Statistics." In *Classification, Data Analysis, and Knowledge Organization*, edited by H.-H. Bock and P. Ihm, 299–310. Berlin: Springer.

Alt, K., W. Vach, K. Frifelt, and M. Kunter. 1995. "Familienanalyse in kupferzeitlichen Kollektivgräbern aus Umm al-Nar; Abu Dhabi." *Arabian Archaeology and Epigraphy* 6:65–80.

Álvarez-Mon, J. 2019. *The Monumental Reliefs of the Elamite Highlands: A Complete Inventory and Analysis (from the Seventeenth to the Sixth Century BC)*. University Park, PA: Eisenbrauns.

Amiet, P. 1973. "La glyptique de la fin de l'Élam." *Arts Asiatiques* 28:3–32.

———. 1979a. "Alternance et dualité: Essai d'interprétation de l'histoire élamite." *Akkadica* 15:2–22.

———. 1979b. "Archaeological Discontinuity and Ethnic Duality in Elam." *Antiquity* 53:195–204.

Andreas, F. C. 1904. "Ueber einige Fragen der ältesten persischen Geschichte." *Verhandlungen des XIII. Internationalen Orientalisten-Kongresses. Hamburg September 1902*, 93–99. Leiden: Brill.

Andree, R. 1889. *Ethnographische Parallelen und Vergleiche*. New ed. Leipzig: Verlag von Veit.

Artin Pacha, Y. 1902. *Contribution à l'étude du blason en Orient*. London: Bernard Quaritch.

Atkinson, K. M. T. 1956. "The Legitimacy of Cambyses and Darius as Kings of Egypt." *JAOS* 76:167–77.

Avery-Quash, S. 2004. "Williams Family (*per. c. 1800–c. 1875*)." *Oxford Dictionary of National Biography*. https://doi.org/10.1093/ref:odnb/72918.

Badamchi, H. 2018a. "Law in a Multicultural Society: Akkadian Legal Texts from Susa in Comparative Perspective." *Elamica* 8:3–12.

———. 2018b. "The Care of the Elderly in Susa: The Akkadian Documents from the Sukkalmah Period." *Akkadica* 139 (2): 159–78.

———. 2019. "According to the Laws Established by the Gods! A Re-examination of MDP 23, 321+322." *ZA* 109:145–54.

Badian, E. 2000. "Darius III." *Harvard Studies in Classical Philology* 100:241–67.

———. 2015. "Sisigambis." *Encyclopædia Iranica*, online edition, www.iranicaonline.org/articles /sisigambis.

Bahadori, A. 2017. "Achaemenid Empire, Tribal Confederations of Southwestern Persia and Seven Families." *IrSt* 50:173–97.

Baladouni, V., and M. Makepeace. 1998. "Armenian Merchants of the Seventeenth and Early Eighteenth Centuries: English East India Company Sources." *Transactions of the American Philosophical Society*, n.s., 88 (4): i–xxxvii, 1–294.

Barth, F. 1961. *Nomads of South Persia: The Basseri Tribe of the Khamseh Confederacy*. Boston: Little, Brown.

———. 1986. "Father's Brother's Daughter Marriage in Kurdistan." *Journal of Anthropological Research* 42:389–96.

Bateni, M. R. 1973. "Kinship Terms in Persian." *Anthropological Linguistics* 15:324–27.

Beaumont, A. de. 1853. *Recherches sur l'origine du blason et en particulier sur la fleur de lis*. Paris: A. Leleux.

Beekes, R. S. P. 1976. "Uncle and Nephew." *Journal of Indo-European Studies* 4:43–63.

Bell, C. H. 1922. "The Sister's Son in the Medieval German Epic." *University of California Publications in Modern Philology* 10 (2): 67–182.

Bengtson, H. 1937. Review of O. Leuze, *Die Satrapieneinteilung in Syrien und im Zweistromlande von 520–320. Gnomon* 13:113–29.

Benveniste, É. 1932. "Les classes sociales dans la tradition avestique." *JA* 221:117–34.

Berberian, M., S. Malek Shahmirzadeh, J. Nokandeh, and M. Djamali. 2012. "Archaeoseismicity and Environmental Crises at the Sialk Mounds, Central Iranian Plateau, since the Early Neolithic." *Journal of Archaeological Science* 39:2845–58.

Berberian, M., C. Petrie, D. T. Potts, A. Asgari Chaverdi, A. Dusting, A. Sardari Zarchi, L. Weeks, P. Ghassemi, and R. Noruzi. 2014. "Archaeoseismicity of the Mounds and Monuments along the Kāzerun Fault (Western Zāgros, SW Iranian Plateau) since the Chalcolithic Period." *IrAnt* 49:1–81.

Bernbeck, R. 1989. *Die neolithische Keramik aus Qale Rostam, Bakhtiyari-Gebiet (Iran): Klassifikation, Produktionsanalyse und Datierungspotential.* Vol. 1. Berlin: Schäuble.

Bichler, R. 2001. *Herodots Welt: Der Aufbau der Historie am Bild der fremden Länder und Völker, ihrer Zivilisationn und ihrer Geschichte.* 2nd ed. Berlin: Akademie.

Bigwood, J. M. 2009. "'Incestuous' Marriage in Achaemenid Iran: Myths and Realities." *Klio* 91:311–41.

Binder, C. 2008. *Plutarchs Vita des Artaxerxes: Ein historischer Kommentar.* Berlin: Walter de Gruyter.

Bivar, A. D. H. 1959. "Details and Devices in Sassanian Sculptures." *Oriental Art* 5:11–14.

———. 1970. Review of W. Hinz, *Altiranische Funde und Forschungen. BSOAS* 33:398–401.

———. 1985. "A Persian Fairyland." In *Papers in Honour of Professor Mary Boyce*, edited by H. W. Bailey, A. D. H. Bivar, J. Duchesne-Guillemin, and J. R. Hinnells, 25–42. Leiden: Acta Iranica 24.

Boas, F. 1940. *Race, Language and Culture.* New York: Macmillan.

Börker-Klähn, J. 1970. "Untersuchungen zur altelamischen Archäologie." PhD diss., Freie Universität, Berlin.

Braganza, V. M. 2022. "'Many Ciphers, Although but One for Meaning': Lady Mary Wroth's Many-Sided Monogram." *English Literary Renaissance* 52:124–52.

Braidwood, R. J. 1958. "Vere Gordon Childe, 1892–1957." *AA* 60:733–36.

Brake, L., and M. Demoor. 2009. *Dictionary of Nineteenth-Century Journalism in Great Britain and Ireland.* Gent: Academia Press and London: British Library.

Brehaut, E. 1916. *History of the Franks by Gregory, Bishop of Tours.* New York: Columbia University Press.

Bremmer, J. 1976. "Avunculate and Fosterage." *Journal of Indo-European Studies* 4:65–78.

Bremmer, R. H. 1980. "The Importance of Kinship: Uncle and Nephew in 'Beowulf.'" *Amsterdamer Beiträge zur älteren Germanistik* 15:21–38.

Brereton, G. 2016. "Mortuary Rites, Economic Behaviour and the Circulation of Goods in the Transition from Village to Urban Life in Early Mesopotamia. *Cambridge Archaeological Journal* 26:191–216.

Briant, P. 1990. "Hérodote et la société perse." In *Hérodote et les peuples non grecs*, edited by G. Nenci and O. Reverdin, 69–104. Vandœuvres-Geneva: Entretiens sur l'Antiquité classique 35.

———. 1996. *Histoire de l'Empire perse de Cyrus à Alexandre.* 2 vols. Leiden: Achaemenid History 10.

Brinkman, J. A. 1968. *A Political History of Post-Kassite Babylonia, 1158–722 B.C.* Rome: Analecta Orientalia 43.

———. 2006. "Babylonian Royal Land Grants, Memorials of Financial Interest, and Invocation of the Divine." *JESHO* 49:1–47.

Bromberg, C. A. 1990. "Sasanian Royal Emblems in Northern Caucasus." In *Proceedings of the First European Conference of Iranian Studies Held in Turin, September 7th–11th, 1987 by the Societas Iranologica Europæa,* vol. 1, edited by G. Gnoli and A. Panaino, 1–17. Rome: SOR 67/1.

Brooks, W. 2009. *Philippe Quinault, Dramatist.* Oxford: Peter Lang.

Brosius, M. 2010. "Women i. In Pre-Islamic Persia." *Encyclopædia Iranica,* online edition, www.iranicaonline.org/articles/women-i.

Bruinessen, M. van. 1992. *Agha, Shaikh and State: The Social and Political Structures of Kurdistan.* London: Zed.

Brundage, B. C. 1956. "Feudalism in Ancient Mesopotamia and Iran." In *Feudalism in History,* edited by R. Coulburn, 93–119. Princeton, NJ: Princeton University Press.

Buchler, I. R. 1964. "A Formal Account of the Hawaiian- and Eskimo-Type Kinship Terminologies." *Southwestern Journal of Anthropology* 20:286–318.

Buckingham, J. S. 1830. *Travels in Assyria, Media, and Persia, including a journey from Bagdad by Mount Zagros, to Hamadan, the ancient Ecbatana, researches in Ispahan and the ruins of Persepolis . . .* Vol. 1. London: Henry Colburn.

Burrows, M. 1940. "The Ancient Oriental Background of Hebrew Levirate Marriage." *BASOR* 77:2–15.

Busse, H. 1972. *History of Persia under Qājār Rule, Translated from the Persian of Ḥasan-E Fasā'i's Fārsnāma-Ye Nāṣeri.* New York: Columbia University Press.

———. 2011. "'Abbās Mīrzā Qājār." *Encyclopædia Iranica,* online edition, www.iranicaonline.org/articles/abbas-mirza-qajar.

Buxtorf, J. 1639. *Lexicon Chaldaicum, Talmudicum et Rabinicum . . .* Basel: Ludwig König.

Caldwell, J. R. 1967. *Investigations at Tal-i-Iblis.* Springfield: Illinois State Museum Preliminary Reports 9.

Cardascia, G. 1983. Lehnswesen B. In der Perserzeit. *RlA* 6:547–50.

Carnoy, A. J. 1917. "Iranian View of Origins in Connection with Similar Babylonian Beliefs." *JAOS* 36:300–320.

Carter, E. 2014. "Royal Women in Elamite Art." In *Extraction & Control: Studies in Honor of Matthew W. Stolper,* edited by M. Kozuh, W. Henkelman, C. E. Jones, and C. Woods, 41–61. Chicago: SAOC 68.

Cecil, E. 1895. *Primogeniture: A Short History of Its Development in Various Countries and Its Practical Effects.* London: John Murray.

Chang, K. C. 1983. *Art, Myth, and Ritual: The Path to Political Authority in Ancient China.* Cambridge, MA: Harvard University Press.

Christensen, A. 1907. *L'empire des Sassanides: Le peuple, l'état, la cour.* Copenhagen: Det Kongelige Danske Videnskabs Selskab Skrifter, 7. Rækker, Historisk og Filosofisk Afdeling 1.1.

———. 1934. Review of G. Hüsing, *Porušātiš und das achamanidische Lehnswesen. OLZ* 37:698–99.

———. 1936. *L'Iran sous les Sassanides*. Copenhagen: Levin & Munksgaard.

Christesen, P. 2006. "Xenophon's *Cyropaedia* and Military Reform in Sparta." *Journal of Hellenic Studies* 126:47–65.

Civil, M. 2003. "Reading Gilgameš II: Gilgameš and Huwawa." In *Literatur, Politik und Recht in Mesopotamien: Festschrift für Claus Wilcke*, edited by W. Sallaberger, K. Volk, and A. Zgoll, 77–86. Wiesbaden: Harrassowitz.

Cleß, K. von. 1864. "Achaemenes." *RE* 1 (1): 43–54.

Codrington, R. H. 1889. "On Social Regulations in Melanesia." *JRAI* 8:306–13.

Colditz, I. 2000. *Zur Sozialterminologie der iranischen Manichäer: Eine semantische Analyse im Vergleich zu den nichtmanichäischen iranischen Quellen*. Wiesbaden: Harrassowitz.

Crawley, A. E. 1907. "Exogamy and the Mating of Cousins." In *Anthropological Essays Presented to E. B. Tylor in Honour of His 75th Birthday, Oct. 2 1907*, edited by H. Balfour et al., 51–63. Oxford: Clarendon Press.

Croucher, K. 2010. "Figuring Out Identity: The Body and Identity in the Ubaid." In *Beyond the Ubaid: Transformation and Integration in the Prehistoric Societies of the Middle East*, edited by R. A. Carter and G. Philip, 113–23. Chicago: SAOC 63.

Csiky, G. 2006. "The *Tuzūkāt-I Tīmūrī* as a Source for Military History." *AOASH* 59:439–91.

Cumont, F. 1924. "Les unions entre proches à Doura et chez les Perses." *Comptes rendus des Séances de l'Académie des Inscriptions et Belles-Lettres* 68:53–62.

Cuq, E. 1931. "Les actes juridiques susiens." *RA* 28:47–71.

Daems, A., and K. Croucher. 2007. "Artificial Cranial Modification in Prehistoric Iran: Evidence from Crania and Figurines." *IrAnt* 42:1–21.

Dalley, S. 1980. "Old Babylonian Dowries." *Iraq* 42:53–74.

Dalton, O. M. 1915. *Catalogue of the Engraved Gems of the Post-Classical Periods in the Department of British and Mediaeval Antiquities and Ethnography in the British Museum*. London: Trustees of the British Museum.

Dandamaev, M. A. 1992. *Iranians in Achaemenid Babylonia*. Costa Mesa, CA: Mazda.

D'Anville, J.-B. B. 1761. "Mémoire sur un Monument très-ancien, sculpté dans une montagne de la Médie." *Histoire de l'Académie Royale des Inscriptions et Belles-Lettres* 27:159–67.

Daryaee, T. 2013. "Marriage, Property and Conversion among the Zoroastrians: From Late Sasanian to Islamic Iran." *Journal of Persianate Societies* 6:91–100.

Davy, W. 1781. *Institutes Political and Military, Written Originally in the Mogul Language, by the Great Timour, Improperly Called Tamerlane . . .* Oxford: Clarendon Press.

De Graef, K. 2012. "Dual Power in Susa: Chronicle of a Transitional Period from Ur III via Šimaški to the Sukkalmas." *BSOAS* 75:525–46.

———. 2019. "It Is You, My Love, You, Who Are the Stranger: Akkadian and Elamite at the Crossroads of Language and Writing." In *A Stranger in the House—the Crossroads III*, edited by J. Mynářová, M. Kilani, and S. Alivernini, 91–120. Prague: Charles University, Faculty of Arts.

De Graef, K., and J. Tavernier, eds. 2013. *Susa and Elam: Archaeological, Philological, Historical and Geographical Perspectives. Proceedings of the International Congress Held at Ghent University, December 14–17, 2009*. Leiden: Brill.

Digard, J.-P. 1975. "Campements Baxtyâri: Observations d'un ethnologue sur des matériaux intéressant l'archéologue." *StIr* 4:117–29.

———. 1987. "Jeux de structures: Segmentarité et pouvoir chez les nomades Baxtyâri d'Iran." *L'Homme* 27:12–53.

Dijk, Jan van. 1986. "Die dynastischen Heiraten zwischen Kassiten und Elamern: Eine verhängnisvolle Politik." *Orientalia* 55:159–70.

Doerfer, G. 2011. "āl tamḡā." *Encyclopædia Iranica*, online edition, www.iranicaonline.org /articles/al-tamga-red-seal.

Dollfus, G., and P. Encrevé. 1982. "Marques sur poteries dans la Susiane du Ve millénaire: Réflexions et comparaisons." *Paléorient* 8 (1): 107–15.

Donnan, H. 1988. *Marriage among Muslims: Preference and Choice in Northern Pakistan.* Leiden: Brill.

Dyson, R. H., Jr. 1965. "Problems in the Relative Chronology of Iran, 6000–2000 BC." In *Chronologies in Old World archaeology*, edited by R. W. Ehrich, 215–56. Chicago: University of Chicago Press.

Eggan, F. 1937. "Historical Changes in the Choctaw Kinship System." *AA* 39:34–52.

Eichwald, E. 1837. *Reise auf dem Caspischen Meere und in den Kaukasus. Unternommen in den Jahren 1825–1826.* Vol. 1, part 2. Stuttgart: J. G. Cotta'schen Buchhandlung.

Eilers, W. 1974. "Die Schere des Kartīr." *Baghdader Mitteilungen* 7:71–83.

———. 1976. "Nochmals zur Schere des Kartīr." *AMI* 9:175–78.

———. 1988. "Banda 'servant.'" *Encyclopædia Iranica*, online edition, www.iranicaonline.org /articles/banda-servant.

Entwistle, C., and N. Adams, eds. 2011. *"Gems of Heaven": Recent Research on Engraved Gemstones in Late Antiquity, c. AD 200–600.* London: British Museum Research Publication 177.

Erdal, M. 1991. *Old Turkic Word Formation. a Functional Approach to the Lexicon.* Vol. 1. Wiesbaden: Harrassowitz.

Erdmann, K. (1943) 1969. *Die Kunst Irans zur Zeit der Sasaniden.* Mainz: Florian Kupferberg.

Ewald, H. 1866. *Die Alterthümer des Volkes Israel.* Göttingen: In der dietrichischen Buchhandlung.

Farnsworth, W. O. 1913. *Uncle and Nephew in the Old French Chansons De Geste: A Study in the Survival of Matriarchy.* New York: Columbia University Press.

Fieux, C. des [Chevalier de Mouhy]. 1780. *Abrégé de l'histoire du théatre françois, depuis son origine jusqu'au premier Juin de l'année 1780.* Vol. 2. Paris: Fieux, Jorry and Mérigot.

Flannery, K. V. 1967. Review of G. R. Willey, *An Introduction to American Archaeology,* vol. 1. *Scientific American* 217:119–22.

Fletcher, J. 2012. *Performing Oaths in Classical Greek Drama.* Cambridge: Cambridge University Press.

Fortes, M. 1953. "The Structure of Unilineal Descent Groups." *AA* 55:17–41.

———. 1959. "Descent, Filiation and Affinity: A Rejoinder to Dr. Leach: Part II." *Man* 331:206–12.

———. 1969. *Kinship and the Social Order: The Legacy of Lewis Henry Morgan.* Chicago: Aldine.

Fortunato, L. 2012. "The Evolution of Matrilineal Kinship Organization." *Proceedings of the Royal Society B* 279:4939–45.

Fortunato, L., C. Holden, and R. Mace. 2006. "From Bridewealth to Dowry? A Bayesian Estimation of Ancestral States of Marriage Transfers in Indo-European Groups." *Human Nature* 17:355–76.

Francis, A. G. 1926. "On a Romano-British Castration Clamp Used in the Rites of Cybele." *Proceedings of the Royal Society of Medicine* 19:95–110.

Frandsen, P. J. 2009. *Incestuous and Close-Kin Marriage in Ancient Egypt and Persia: An Examination of the Evidence.* Copenhagen: CNIP 34.

Frazer, J. G. 1935. *Totemism and Exogamy: A Treatise on Certain Early Forms of Superstition and Society.* Vol. 2. London: Macmillan.

Frémion, C. A. F., and J. M. Soulerin. 1834. *Valère Maxime, faits et paroles mémorables.* Paris: C. L. F. Panckoucke.

Frye, R. N. 1963. Review of R. Göbl, *Die Münzen der Sasaniden im königlichen Münzkabinett, Haag. Artibus Asiae* 26:176.

———. 1970. Review of H. Humbach, *Baktrische Sprachdenkmäler. Indo-Iranian Journal* 12 (4): 263–66.

———. 1987. "Feudalism in Sasanian and Early Islamic Iran." *Jerusalem Studies in Arabic and Islam* 9:13–18.

Fuchs, A. 2003. Review of Waters, *A Survey of Neo-Elamite History. ZA* 93:128–37.

Fürstenthal, R. J. 1842. *Das jüdische Traditionswesen, dargestellt in des R. Moses Maimonides Einleitung in seinen Mischnahkommentar, namentlich zur Mischnahordnung Seraim.* Breslau.

Gall, H. von. 1972. "Persische und medische Stämme." *AMI* 5:261–83.

———. 1990. *Das Reiterkampfbild in der iranischen und iranisch beeinflußten Kunst parthischer und sasanidischer Zeit.* Berlin: Teheraner Forschungen 6.

Garbáty, T. J. 1977. "The Uncle-Nephew Motif: New Light on Its Origin and Development." *Folklore* 88:220–35.

Gatterer, J. C. 1798. *Abriß der Diplomatik.* Göttingen: Vandenhoeck and Ruprecht.

Gazerani, S. 2016. *The Sistani Cycle of Epics and Iran's National History.* Leiden: Brill.

Geertz, C. 1964. "Teknonymy in Bali: Parenthood, Age-Grading and Genealogical Amnesia." *JRAI* 94:94–108.

Geiger, W. 1882. *Ostiranische Kultur im Altertum.* Erlangen: Andreas Deichert.

Gennep, A. van. 1902. "Les 'wasm,' ou marques de propriété des Arabes." *Internationales Archiv für Ethnographie* 15:85–98.

———. 1905. "Notes sur l'héraldisation de la marque de propriété et les origines du blason." *Bulletins et mémoires de la Société d'Anthropologie de Paris* (5th ser.) 6:103–12.

Ghirshman, R. 1946. "Fīrūzābād." *BIFAO* 46:1–28.

———. 1956. *Bîchâpour.* Vol. 2, *Les mosaïques sassanides.* Paris: Librairie Orientaliste Paul Geuthner.

Glassner, J.-J. 1994. "Ruḫušak—mār aḫatim: La transmission du pouvoir en Élam." *Journal Asiatique* 282:219–36.

Gnoli, G. 1989. *The Idea of Iran: An Essay on Its Origin.* Rome: SOR 62.

Göbl, R. 1967. *Dokumente zur Geschichte der iranischen Hunnen in Baktrien und Indien.* Vol. 2. Wiesbaden: Harrassowitz.

———. 1971. "Die sasanidischen Tonbullen vom Takht-i-Suleiman und die Probleme der sasanidischen Sphragistik." *AAASH* 19:95–112.

———. 1976. *Die Tonbullen vom Tacht-e Suleiman: Ein Beitrag zur spätsasanidischen Sphragistik.* Berlin: Dietrich Reimer.

Goldberg, J. 2004. "The Berlin Letter, Middle Elamite Chronology and Šutruk-Nahhunte I's Genealogy." *IrAnt* 39:33–42.

Goldsmid, F. J. 1880. "Persia; and Its Military Resources." *Journal of the Royal United Service Institution* 23:149–72.

Goody, J. 1956. "A Comparative Approach to Incest and Adultery." *British Journal of Sociology* 7:286–305.

———. 1969. "Adoption in Cross-Cultural Perspective." *Comparative Studies in Society and History* 11:55–78.

Goody, J., and S. J. Tambiah. 1973. *Bridewealth and Dowry*. Cambridge: Cambridge University Press.

Gorris, E. 2014. "Power and Politics in the Neo-Elamite Kingdom." 2 vols. PhD diss., Université catholique de Louvain.

Gourley, D. R., and D. J. Johnson. 2016. "Nabataean Amethyst Trade: Sources, Production, and Use." In *Studies on Nabataean Culture II*, edited by N. I. Khairy, A. Accettola, Z. al-Salameen, R. A. Brandmeier, and S. A. D. Farajat, 25–52. Amman: Publications of the Deanship of Scientific Research, University of Jordan.

Grafton, A. 1999. "Jean Hardouin: The Antiquary as Pariah." *Journal of the Warburg and Courtauld Institutes* 62:241–67.

Grätz, S. 2004. *Das Edikt des Artaxerxes: Eine Untersuchung zum religionspolitischen und historischen Umfeld von Esra 7, 12–26*. Berlin: de Gruyter.

Graves, R. 1935. *Claudius the God and His Wife Messalina*. New York: Harrison Smith and Robert Haas.

Gray, L. H. 1915. "Marriage (Iranian)." *Encyclopaedia of Religion and Ethics* 8:456–59.

Grayson, A. K. 1975. *Assyrian and Babylonian Chronicles*. Locust Valley, NY: Texts from Cuneiform Sources 5.

Greengus, S. 1990. "Bridewealth in Sumerian Sources." *Hebrew Union College Annual* 61:25–88.

Greenspahn, F. E. 1994. *When Brothers Dwell Together: The Preeminence of Younger Siblings in the Hebrew Bible*. New York: Oxford University Press.

Grenet, F. 2011. "Quelques nouvelles notes sur Kerdīr et 'sa' vision." In *Rabbo l'olmyn: Florilège offert à Philippe Gignoux pour son 80ᵉ anniversaire*, edited by R. Gyselen and C. Jullien, 123–39. Paris: Cahiers de *Studia Iranica* 43.

Griffith, R. D. 2009. "Honeymoon Salad: Cambyses' Uxoricide According to the Egyptians (Hdt. 3.32.3–4)." *Historia* 58:131–40.

———. 2011. "An Offer You Can't Retract: Xerxes' Nod and Masistes' Wife (Herodotus 9.111.1)." *Classical Quarterly*, n.s., 61:310–12.

Grillot, F. 1988. "A propos d'un cas de 'lévirat' élamite." *JA* 276:61–70.

Gros, É. 1970. *Philippe Quinault, sa vie et son œuvre*. Geneva: Slatkine Reprints.

Gummere, F. J. 1901. "The Sister's Son." In *An English Miscellany: Presented to Dr. Furnivall in Honour of His Seventy-Fifth Birthday*, 133–49. Oxford: Clarendon Press.

Gyselen, R. 1989. *La Géographie administrative de l'Empire sassanide: Les témoignages sigillographiques*. Paris: Res Orientales 1.

———. 2006. *Sasanian Seals and Sealings in the A. Saeedi Collection*. Louvain: Acta Iranica 44.

Gyselen, R., and Y. Monsef. 2012. "Décryptage de noms propres sur des monogrammes sassanides." In *Objets et documents inscrits en pārsīg*, edited by R. Gyselen, 149–78. Leuven: Res Orientales 21.

Hall, E. 1989. *Inventing the Barbarian: Greek Self-Definition through Tragedy*. Oxford: Clarendon Press.

Hallock, R. T. 1969. *Persepolis Fortification Tablets*. Chicago: Oriental Institute of the University of Chicago.

Hallock, R. T. 1978. "Selected Fortification Tablets." *Cahiers de la délégation française en Iran* 8:109–136.

Hammer, J. von. 1819. "Ueber die Geographie Persiens." *Jahrbücher der Literatur* 7:197–300.

Hancock, C. F. 1857. *Illustrated and Descriptive Catalogue of the Celebrated Devonshire Gems from the Collection of the Duke of Devonshire, K. G., arranged and mounted for His Grace, as a Parure of Jewels.* Westminster: T. Brettell.

Hansson, U. R. 2014. "'Ma passion . . . ma folie dominante': Stosch, Winckelmann, and the Allure of the Engraved Gems of the Ancients." *MDCCC 1800* 3:13–31.

Harper, P. O. 1974. "Sasanian Medallion Bowls with Human Busts." In *Near Eastern Numismatics, Iconography, Epigraphy and History: Studies in Honor of George C. Miles,* edited by D. K. Kouymjian, 61–81. Beirut: American University of Beirut.

———. 1978. *The Royal Hunter: Art of the Sasanian Empire.* New York: Asia Society.

Harrell, J. A., S. E. Sidebotham, R. S. Bagnall, S. Marchand, J. E. Gates, and J.-L. Rivard. 2006. "The Ptolemaic to Early Roman Amethyst Quarry at Abu Diyeiba in Egypt's Eastern Desert." *Bulletin de l'Institut français d'archéologie orientale* 106:127–62.

Harris, L. J., J. Carbone, L. E. Teitelbaum, and R. Rebouché. 2018. *Family Law.* 6th ed. New York: Wolters Kluwer.

Hazewindus, M. W. 2004. *When Women Interfere: Studies of the Role of Women in Herodotus' Histories.* Leiden: Amsterdam Studies in Classical Philology 12.

Held, J. 1863. *Staat und Gesellschaft vom Standpunkte der Geschichte der Menschheit und des Staats.* Vol. 2. Leipzig: F. A. Brockhaus.

Hellmann, S., and M. Palyi. 1923. *Wirtschaftsgeschichte von Max Weber. Abriss der universalen Sozial- und Wirtschafts-Geschichte aus den nachgelassenen Vorlesungen.* Munich: Duncker & Humblot.

Helm, P. 1981. "Herodotus' *Mêdikos logos* and Median History." *Iran* 19:85–90.

Henkelman, W. F. M. 2003. "An Elamite Memorial: The Šumar of Cambyses and Hystaspes." In *A Persian Perspective: Essays in Memory of Heleen Sancisi-Weerdenburg,* edited by W. Henkelman and A. Kuhrt, 101–72. Leiden: Achaemenid History 13.

———. 2010a. "'Consumed before the King': The Table of Darius, That of Irdabama and Irtaštuna, and That of His Satrap, Karkiš." In *Der Achämenidenhof / The Achaemenid Court,* edited by B. Jacobs and R. Rollinger, 667–775. Wiesbaden: Harrassowitz.

———. 2010b. "Xerxes, Atossa and the Persepolis Fortification Archive." *Annual Report of the Netherlands Institute for the Near East/Leiden, Netherlands Institute in Turkey/Istanbul 2010:* 27–33.

———. 2011. "Cyrus the Persian and Darius the Elamite: A Case of Mistaken Identity." In *Herodot und das Persische Weltreich / Herodotus and the Persian Empire,* edited by R. Rollinger, B. Truschnegg, and R. Bichler, 577–634. Wiesbaden: Harrassowitz.

Henkelman, W. F. M., and K. Kleber. 2007. "Babylonian Workers in the Persian Heartland: Palace Building at Matannan during the Reign of Cambyses." In *Persian Responses: Political and Cultural Interaction with(in) the Achaemenid Empire,* edited by C. Tuplin, 163–76. Swansea: Classical Press of Wales.

Herlihy, D. 1970. *The History of Feudalism.* New York: Palgrave Macmillan.

Herrenschmidt, C. 1987. "Notes sur la parenté chez les Perses au début de l'empire Achéménide." In *Achaemenid History II. The Greek Sources,* edited by H. Sancisi-Weerdenburg and A. Kuhrt, 53–67. Leiden: Nederlands Instituut voor het Nabije Oosten.

Herzfeld, E. 1924. *Paikuli: Monuments and Inscriptions of the Early History of the Sasanian Empire*, 2 vols. Berlin: Dietrich Reimer.

———. 1926. "Reisebericht." *ZDMG* 80:225–84.

———. 1928. "La sculpture rupestre de la Perse sassanide." *Revue des arts asiatiques* 5:129–42.

———. 1937. "Old-Iranian 'Peership.'" *BSOAS* 8:937–45.

———. 1938a. *Altpersische Inschriften*. Berlin: AMI Ergänzungsband 1.

———. 1938b. "Khusrau Parwēz und der Ṭāq i Vastān." *AMI* 9:91–158.

———. 1968. *The Persian Empire*. Wiesbaden: Franz Steiner.

Hinz, W. 1962. "Die elamischen Inschriften des Hanne." In *A Locust's Leg: Studies in Honour of S. H. Taqizadeh*, edited by W. B. Henning and E. Yarshater, 105–15. London: Percy Lund, Humphries.

———. 1964. *Das Reich Elam*. Stuttgart: Urban-Bücher 82.

———. 1969. *Altiranische Funde und Forschungen*. Berlin: De Gruyter.

Hirt, A. M. 2010. *Imperial Mines and Quarries in the Roman World: Organizational Aspects 27 BC–AD 235*. Oxford: Oxford University Press.

Hjerrild, B. 2003. *Studies in Zoroastrian Family Law: A Comparative Analysis*. Copenhagen: CNIP 28.

———. 2006. "Succession and Kinship in the Late Sasanian Era." In *Proceedings of the 5th Conference of the Societas Iranologica Europæa Held in Ravenna, 6–11 October 2003*, vol. 1, edited by A. Panaino and A. Piras, 479–84. Milan: Mimesis.

Hoffmann, I. 1981. "Kambyses in Ägypten." *Studien zur Altägyptischen Kultur* 9:179–99.

Hoffmann, I., and A. Vorbichler. 1980. "Das Kambysesbild bei Herodot." *Archiv für Orientforschung* 27:86–105.

Hole, F., K. V. Flannery, and J. A. Neely. 1969. *Prehistory and Human Ecology of the Deh Luran Plain: An Early Village Sequence from Khuzistan, Iran*. Ann Arbor: Memoirs of the Museum of Anthropology, University of Michigan 1.

Homeyer, C. G. 1870. *Die Haus- und Hofmarken*. Berlin: Verlag der königlichen geheimen Ober-Hofbuchdruckerei.

Horn, P., and G. Steindorff. 1891. *Sassanidische Siegelsteine*. Berlin: Mittheilungen aus den Orientalischen Sammlungen der Königliche Museen zu Berlin 4.

How, W. W., and J. Wells. 1912. *A Commentary on Herodotus*. Vol. 2. Oxford: Clarendon Press.

Hübschmann, H. 1889. "Ueber die persische Verwandtenheirath." *ZDMG* 43:308–12.

———. 1897. *Armenische Grammatik*. Vol. 1. Leipzig: Bibliothek indogermanischer Grammatiken 6.

Hüsing, G. 1905. "Hadamdun." *OLZ* 8:248–50.

———. 1933. *Porušātiš und das achamanidische Lehenswesen*. 2nd ed. Vienna: Bausteine zur Geschichte, Völkerkunde und Mythenkunde Ergänzungsheft 2.

Hyland, J. 2018. "Hystaspes, Gobryas, and Elite Marriage Politics in Teispid Persia." *Dabir* 5:30–35.

Jackson, A. V. W. 1920. *Early Persian Poetry, from the Beginnings down to the Time of Firdausi*. New York: Macmillan.

Jacobson, D. M. 2014. "Herod the Great's Royal Monogram." *Israel Numismatic Research* 9:95–101.

Jahn, K. 1969. *Die Geschichte der Oġuzen des Rašīd ad-Dīn*. Vienna: Denkschriften der Österreichischen Akademie der Wissenschaften, phil.-hist. Kl. 100.

Jänichen, H. 1956. *Bildzeichen der königlichen Hoheit bei den iranischen Völkern*. Bonn: Antiquitas Reihe 1/3.

Jansen-Winkeln, K. 1999. Gab es in der altägyptischen Geschichte eine feudalistische Epoche? *Die Welt des Orients* 30:7–20.

Jochelson, W. 1928. *Peoples of Asiatic Russia*. New York: American Museum of Natural History.

Jodrell, R. P. 1822. *The Persian Heroine: A Tragedy*. London: Samuel and Richard Bentley.

Johnson, J. 1818. *A Journey from India to England, through Persia, Georgia, Russia, Poland, and Prussia, in the Year 1817*. London: Longman, Hurst, Rees, Orme, and Brown.

Jones, C. P. 1996. "ἔθνος and γένος in Herodotus." *Classical Quarterly* 46:315–20.

Justi, C. 1871. *Antiquarische Briefe des Baron Philipp von Stosch*. Marburg: C. L. Pfeil.

Justi, F. 1895. *Iranisches Namenbuch*. Marburg: N. G. Elwert'sche Verlagsbuchhandlung.

Kaim, B. 2009. "Investiture or Mithra. Towards a New Interpretation of So Called Investiture Scenes in Parthian and Sasanian Art." *IrAnt* 44:403–13.

Kalb, D., H. Marks, and H. Tak. 1996. "Historical Anthropology and Anthropological History: Two Distinct Programs." *Focaal* 26/27:5–13.

Karras-Klapproth, M. 1988. *Prosopographische Studien zur Geschichte des Partherreiches auf der Grundlage antiker literarischer Überlieferung*. Bonn: Habelt.

Keiper, P. 1879. "Atossa nach Äschylus 'Persern' und nach Herodot." *Blätter für das Bayerische Gymnasial- und Real-Schulwesen* 15:6–22.

Kent, R. G. 1946. "The Oldest Old Persian Inscriptions." *JAOS* 66:206–12.

———. 1950. *Old Persian: Grammar, Texts, Lexicon*. New Haven, CT: American Oriental Society.

Ker Porter, R. 1821. *Travels in Georgia, Persia, Armenia, Ancient Babylonia, &c. &c. during the Years 1817, 1818, 1819, and 1820*. Vol. 1. London: Longman, Hurst, Rees, Orme, and Brown.

King, C. W. 1872. *Antique Gems and Rings*. 2 vols. London: Bell and Daldy.

Klíma, J. 1963. "Le droit élamite au I^ème millénaire av. n.è. et sa position envers le droit babylonien." *Archiv Orientální* 31:287–309.

Klíma, O. 2016. "Bahrām IV." *Encyclopædia Iranica*, online edition, www.iranicaonline.org/articles/bahram-04.

Klinkott, H. 2005. *Der Satrap. Ein achaimenidischer Amtsträger und seine Handlungsspielräume*. Frankfurt: Oikumene 1.

König, F. W. 1924. "Altpersische Adelsgeschlechter. I: Die Dātuhijān." *WZKM* 31:287–309.

———. 1926a. "Mutterrecht und Thronfolge im alten Elam." In *Festschrift der Nationalbibliothek in Wien herausgegeben zur Feier des 200jährigen Bestehens des Gebäudes*, 529–52. Vienna: Druck und Verlag der Österreichischen Staatsdruckerei.

———. 1926b. "Altpersische Adelsgeschlechter. II: Die Wṛkānijān." *WZKM* 33:23–56.

———. 1938. *Der falsche Bardija: Dareios der Grosse und die Lügenkönige*. Vienna: Klotho 4.

———. 1964. "Geschwisterehe in Elam." *RlA* 3:224–31.

———. 1965. *Die elamischen Königsinschriften*. Graz: Archiv für Orientforschung.

Konstantopoulos, G. V. 2015. "They Are Seven: Demons and Monsters in the Mesopotamian Textual and Artistic Tradition." PhD diss., University of Michigan.

Kornemann, E. 1925. "Zur Geschwisterehe im Altertum." *Klio* 19:355–61.

Korošec, V. 1964. "Keilschriftrecht." In *Orientalisches Recht*, edited by B. Spuler, 49–219. Leiden: HdO 1. Ergänzungsband 3.

Koschaker, P. 1932. Review of Scheil, MDP 22. *OLZ* 35:318–21.

———. 1933. "Fratriarchat, Hausgemeinschaft und Mutterrecht in Keilschriftrechten." *ZA* 41:1–89.

——. 1934. Review of Scheil, MDP 23 and 24. *OLZ* 37:501–3.

——. 1935a. "Gottliches und weltliches Recht nach den Urkunden aus Susa: Zugleich ein Beitrag zu ihrer Chronologie." *Orientalia* 4:38–80.

——. 1935b. "Keilschriftrecht." *ZDMG* 89:1–39.

——. 1936. "Adoptio in fratrem." In *Studi in onore Salvatore Riccobono*. Vol. 3, 361–76. Palermo: G. Castiglia.

——. 1941. Review of Scheil, MDP 28. *OLZ* 44:213–17.

Kramer, C. 1985. "Ceramic Ethnoarchaeology." *Annual Review of Anthropology* 14:77–102.

Kuhrt, A. 2007. *The Persian Empire: A Corpus of Sources from the Achaemenid Period.* Abingdon, UK: Routledge.

Kuper, A. 1985. "The Development of Lewis Henry Morgan's Evolutionism." *Journal of the History of the Behavioral Sciences* 21:3–22.

——. 2008. "Changing the Subject—about Cousin Marriage, among Other Things." *Journal of the Royal Anthropological Institute* 14:717–35.

La Bléterie, J.-P.-R. 1755. *Description de la Germanie et des mœurs de ses habitans, par Tacite.* Vol. 1. Paris: Chez Duchesne.

Lafont, S. 1998. "Fief et féodalité dans le Proche-Orient ancien." In *Les féodalités*, edited by E. Bournazel and J.-P. Poly, 515–630. Paris: Presses universitaires de France.

——. 1999. *Femmes, droit et justice dans l'Antiquité orientale: Contribution à l'étude du droit pénal au Proche-Orient ancien.* Fribourg: OBO 165.

Lambert, W. G. 1991. "The Akkadianization of Susiana under the Sukkalmaḫs." In *Mésopotamie et Elam*, edited by L. De Meyer and H. Gasche, 53–57. Gent: Mesopotamian History and Environment Occasional Publications 1.

Lang, M. L. 1984. *Herodotean Narrative and Discourse.* Cambridge, MA: Harvard University Press.

Langlès, L. 1787. *Instituts politiques et militaires de Tamerlan, proprement appellée Timour . . .* Paris: Chez Née de la Rochelle, Lottin de S.-Germain and Didot fils aîné.

Langsdorff, A., and D. E. McCown. 1942. *Tall-i-Bakun A: Season of 1932.* Chicago: Oriental Institute of the University of Chicago.

Larson, S. 2006. "Kandaules' Wife, Masistes' Wife: Herodotus' Narrative Strategy in Suppressing Names of Women (Hdt. 1.8–12 and 9.108–13)." *Classical Journal* 101:225–44.

Laufer, B. 1917. "The Reindeer and Its Domestication." *Memoirs of the American Anthropological Association* 4:91–150.

Laurent, F. 1861. *Histoire de droit des gens et des relations internationales.* 2nd rev. ed. Vol. 1. Brussels: Meline, Cans.

Leach, E. R. 1951. "The Structural Implications of Matrilateral Cross-Cousin Marriage." *JRAI* 81:23–55.

——. 1977. "The Atom of Kinship, Filiation and Descent: Error in Translation or Confusion of Ideas?" *L'homme* 17:127–29.

Leavitt, G. C. 2013. "Tylor vs. Westermarck: Explaining the Incest Taboo." *Sociology Mind* 3:45–51.

Lecoq, P. 1997. *Les inscriptions de la Perse achémenide.* Paris: Gallimard.

Leeuwen, M. H. D. van, and I. Maas. 2005. "Endogamy and Social Class in History: An Overview." In *Marriage Choices and Class Boundaries: Social Endogamy in History*, edited by M. H. D. van Leeuwen, I. Maas, and A. Miles, 1–23. Cambridge: International Review of Social History Supplement 13.

Lenfant, D. 2004. *Ctésias de Cnide: La Perse, l'Inde, autres fragments.* Paris: Les Belles Lettres.

Lerner, J. A., and P. O. Skjærvø. 2006. "The Seal of a Eunuch in the Sasanian Court." *Journal of Inner Asian Art and Archaeology* 1:115–17.

Lewcock, R. B. 1986. *Wādī Ḥaḍramawt and the Walled City of Shibām.* New York: UNESCO.

Lewer, H. W. 1917. "Samuel Williams of Colchester, Wood Engraver and Painter." *Essex Review* 26 (Oct.): 165–73.

Lewis, T. 1725. *Origines Hebrææ: The Antiquities of the Hebrew Republic.* Vol. 3. London: Sam. Illidge and John Hooke.

Lockhart, L. 1958. *The Fall of the Safavī Dynasty and the Afghan Occupation of Persia.* Cambridge: Cambridge University Press.

Lorentz, K. O. 2010. "Ubaid Headshaping: Negotiations of Identity through Physical Appearance?" In *Beyond the Ubaid: Transformation and Integration in the Prehistoric Societies of the Middle East,* edited by R. A. Carter and G. Philip, 125–48. Chicago: SAOC 63.

Lowie, R. H. 1918. "Survivals and the Historical Method." *American Journal of Sociology* 23:529–35.

Lüle, Ç. 2011. "Non-destructive Gemmological Tests for the Identification of Ancient Gems." In Entwistle and Adams 2011, 1–3.

Macan, R. W. 1908. *Herodotus. The Seventh, Eighth, & Ninth Books . . .* Vol. 1, pt. 2. London: Macmillan.

Mackenzie, D. N. 1999. *Iranica Diversa.* Vol. 1. Rome: SOR 84.

Macuch, M. 1991. "Inzest im vorislamischen Iran." *AMI* 24:141–54.

———. 2003. "Zoroastrian Principles and the Structure of Kinship in Sasanian Iran." In *Religious Themes and Texts of Pre-Islamic Iran and Central Asia,* edited by C. G. Cereti et al., 231–45. Wiesbaden: Harrassowitz.

———. 2007. "The Pahlavi Model Marriage Contract in the Light of Sasanian Family Law." In *Iranian Languages and Texts from Iran and Turan: Ronald E. Emmerick Memorial Volume,* edited by M. Macuch, M. Maggi, and W. Sundermann, 183–204. Wiesbaden: Harrassowitz.

———. 2010. "Incestuous Marriage in the Context of Sasanian Family Law." In *Ancient and Middle Iranian Studies: Proceedings of the Sixth European Conference of Iranian Studies of the Societas Iranologica Europaea in Vienna, Sept. 19–22, 2007,* edited by M. Macuch, D. Weber, and D. Durkin-Meisterernst, 133–48. Wiesbaden: Harrassowitz.

———. 2014. "Ardashir's Genealogy Revisited." *Iran Nameh* 29 (2): 80–94.

———. 2017. "Descent and Inheritance in Zoroastrian and Shi'ite Law: A Preliminary Study." *Der Islam* 94:322–35.

Maksymiuk, K. 2015. "The Parthian Nobility in Xusrō I Anōšīrvān's Court." In *Elites in the Ancient World.* Vol. 2, edited by P. Briks, 189–98. Szczecin: Wydawnictwo Naukowe WH.

Malinowski, B. 1926. *Myth in Primitive Psychology.* London: Kegan Paul, Trench, Trubner.

Manassero, N. 2013. "Tamgas, a Code of the Steppes. Identity Marks and Writing among the Ancient Iranians." *Silk Road* 11:60–69.

Marchesi, G. 2013. "Ur-Nammâ(k)'s Conquest of Susa." In De Graef and Tavernier 2013, 285–91.

Mariette, P. J. 1750. *Traité des Pierres gravées.* Vol. 1. Paris: Imprimerie de l'auteur.

Marquart, J. 1895. "Beiträge zur Geschichte und Sage von Erān." *ZDMG* 49:628–72.

Matsushima, E. 2016. "Women in Elamite Royal Inscriptions: Some Observations." In *The Role of Women in Work and Society in the Ancient Near East,* edited by B. Lion and C. Michel, 416–28. Berlin: SANER 13.

Matthiae, C. 1699. *Theatrum historicum theoretico-practicum: Das ist: Nutz- und Lehrreicher historischer Schauplatz auff welchem die vier grossen Monarchien der Welt als nemlich die chaldäisch-Assyrische oder Babylonische, die Medo-Persische, die Griechische und die Römische* . . . Frankfurt: Johan Jost Erythropel.

McCown, D. E. 1942. *The Comparative Stratigraphy of Early Iran.* Chicago: SAOC 23.

McLennan, J. 1865. *Primitive Marriage.* Edinburgh: Adam and Charles Black.

McPhee, B. 2018. "A Mad King in a Mad World: The Death of Cambyses in Herodotus." *Histos* 12:71–96.

Meillet, A. 1925. *Trois conférences sur les Gâthâ de l'Avesta.* Paris: Annales du Musée Guimet 44.

Menasce, J. de. 1959. "Déchiffrement de motifs alphabétiques de l'Époque sassanide." *BIFAO* 59:309–14.

Meredith, D. 1957. "Inscriptions from the Amethyst Mines at Abu Diyeiba (Eastern Desert of Egypt)." *EOS: Commentarii Societatis Philologae Polonorum* 48 (2): 117–19.

Meyermann, G. 1904. *Göttinger Hausmarken und Familienwappen: Nach den Siegeln des Göttinger städtischen Archivs.* Göttingen: Lüder Borstmann.

Michaelis, J. D. 1786. *Abhandlung von den Ehegesetzen Mosis welche die Heyrathen in die nahe Freundschaft untersagen.* 2nd rev. ed. Frankfurt and Leipzig: n.p.

———. 1793. *Mosaisches Recht.* Vol. 2. 3rd rev. ed. Frankfurt: Johann Gottlieb Garbe.

Mielziner, M. 1902. *The Jewish Law of Marriage and Divorce in Ancient and Modern Times, and Its Relation to the Law of the State.* 2nd rev. ed. New York: Block Publishing.

Mofidi-Nasrabadi, B. 2011. "Die Glyptik aus Haft Tappeh: Interkulturelle Aspekte zur Herrstellung und Benutzung von Siegeln der Anfangsphase der mittelelamischen Zeit." *Elamica* 1:1–347.

———. 2018. "Elam in the Middle Elamite Period." In *The Elamite World,* edited by J. Álvarez-Mon, G. P. Basello, and Y. Wicks, 232–48. London: Routledge.

Moghaddam, A. 2016. "A Fifth Millennium BC Cemetery in the North Persian Gulf: The Zohreh Prehistoric Project." *Antiquity* 90 (353): e3. doi:10.15184/aqy.2016.166.

———. 2018. *A Six Thousand Year Old Sanctuary at Tol-E Chega Sofla.* Tehran: Research Institute for Cultural Heritage and Tourism.

———. 2020. *A Sanctuary at Tol-E Chega Sofla.* Tehran: Research Institute for Cultural Heritage and Tourism.

Montesquieu, C. de S. 1845. *Esprit des lois.* Paris: Librairie de Firmin Didot Frères.

Moore, S. F. 1964. "Descent and Symbolic Filiation." *AA* 66:1308–20.

Mordtmann, A. D. 1876. "Sassanidische Gemmen." *ZDMG* 29:199–211.

Morgan, J. de. 1914. "Feudalism in Persia: Its Origin, Development, and Present Condition." *Annual Report of the Board of Regents of the Smithsonian Institution . . . for the Year Ending 30 June 1913:* 579–606.

Morgan, L. H. 1868. "A Conjectural Solution of the Origin of the Classificatory System of Relationship." *Proceedings of the American Academy of Arts and Sciences* 7:436–77.

———. 1877. *Ancient Society; or, Researches in the Lines of Human Progress from Savagery, through Barbarism to Civilization.* New York: Henry Holt.

Müller, C. W. 2006. *Legende—Novelle—Roman: Dreizehn Kapitel zur erzählenden Prosaliteratur der Antike.* Göttingen: Vandenhoeck & Ruprecht.

Murdock, G. P. 1940. "Double Descent." *AA* 42:555–61.

Natter, L. 1754. *A Treatise on the Ancient Method of Engraving on Precious Stones, Compared with the Modern.* London: Printed for the Author, in Vine-Street, Piccadilly.

Neuhaus, O. 1902. "Der Vater der Sisygambis (und das Verwandtschaftsverhältniss des Dareios III Kodomanos zu Artaxerxes II und III)." *Rheinisches Museum* 57:610–23.

Nickel, H. 1973. "Tamgas and Runes, Magic Numbers and Magic Symbols." *Metropolitan Museum Journal* 8:165–73.

Niebuhr, C. 1778. *Reisebeschreibung nach Arabien und andern umliegenden Ländern.* Vol. 2. Copenhagen: Hofbuchdruckerey bey Nicolaus Möller.

Nielsen, J. P. 2011. *Sons and Descendants: A Social History of Kin Groups and Family Names in the Early Neo-Babylonian Period, 747–626 BC.* Leiden: Culture and History of the Ancient Near East 43.

Nitze, W. A. 1912. "The Sister's Son and the Conte Del Graal." *Modern Philology* 9:291–322.

Nöldeke, T. 1879. *Geschichte der Perser und Araber zur Zeit der Sasaniden, aus der arabischen Chronik des Tabari.* Leiden: Brill.

Oberling, P. 1964. "The Tribes of Qarāca Dāğ: A Brief History." *Oriens* 17:60–95.

Ó Cathasaigh, T. 1986. "The Sister's Son in Early Irish Literature." *Peritia* 5:128–60.

Oers, L. 2010. "A Round Peg in a Square Hole? The Sikkatu in Old Babylonian Susa." *Akkadica* 131:121–43.

———. 2013. "To Invest in Harvest Field Leases in Old Babylonian Susa." *Zeitschrift für Altorientalische und Biblische Rechtsgeschichte* 19:155–69.

Olbrycht, M. J. 2016. "Dynastic Connections in the Arsacid Empire and the Origins of the House of Sāsān." In *The Parthian and Early Sasanian Empires: Adaptation and Expansion,* edited by V. S. Curtis, E. J. Pendleton, M. Alram, and T. Daryaee, 23–35. Oxford: British Institute of Persian Studies.

Olmstead, A. T. E. 1951. *History of Assyria.* Chicago: University of Chicago Press.

Orlov, V. P. 2018. "Persian Aristocracy in the Achaemenid Empire: Social Status (on the Meaning of the Term *Bandakā*)." *Journal of Historical, Philological and Cultural Studies* 4:61–77 (in Russian).

Ouseley, W. 1801. *Observations on Some Medals and Gems Bearing Inscriptions in the Pahlavi or Ancient Persick Character.* London: Oriental Press.

Pallas, P. S. 1776. *Samlungen historischer Nachrichten über die mongolischen Völkerschaften.* Vol. 1. St. Petersburg: Kayserlichen Akademie der Wissenschaften.

Parfaict, F. 1746. *Histoire du theatre françois, depuis son origine jusqu'à présent . . .* Vol. 8. Paris: Le Mercier and Saillant.

Paris, G. 1865. *Histoire poétique de Charlemagne.* Paris: Librairie A. Franck.

Paulus, S. 2013. "Beziehungen zweier Großmächte—Elam und Babylonien in der 2. Hälfte des 2. Jt. v. Chr. Ein Beitrag zur internen Chronologie." In De Graef and Tavernier 2013, 429–49.

Pellerin, J. 1767. *Troisième Supplément aux six volumes de Recueils des Médailles de Rois, de Villes, &c. Publiés en 1762, 1763 & 1765, avec des observations et des corrections.* Paris: L. F. Delatour.

Perikhanian, A. 1983. "Iranian Society and Law." In *The Cambridge History of Iran.* Vol. 3, part 2, *The Seleucid, Parthian and Sasanian Periods,* edited by E. Yarshater, 627–80. Cambridge: Cambridge University Press.

Petit, T. 1990. *Satrapes et satrapies dans l'Empire achéménide de Cyrus le Grand à Xerxès Ier.* Paris: Bibliothèque de la Faculté de Philosophie et Lettres de l'Université de Liège 254.

———. 2004. "Xénophon et la vassalité achéménide." In *Xenophon and His World,* edited by C. Tuplin, 175–99. Stuttgart: Historia-Einzelschrift 172.

Pietrzak, A. 2018. "*Fameux amateur* Philipp von Stosch and the unknown provenance of lost old-masters' drawings from the collection of Count Stanisław Kostka Potocki." *Polish Libraries* 6:115–63.

Pinches, T. G. 1884. "The Babylonian Kings of the Second Period, about 2232 B.C., to the End of the Existence of the Kingdom." *Proceedings of the Society of Biblical Archaeology* 6:193–204.

Pocock, E. 1655. *Porta Mosis sive, dissertationes aliquot à R. Mose Maimonides, suis in varias Mishnaioth, sive textus Talmudici partes . . .* Oxford: H. Hall.

Posener, G. 1936. *La première domination perse en Égypte.* Cairo: Imprimerie de l'Institut français d'archéologie orientale.

Potts, D. T. 1981. "The Potter's Marks of Tepe Yahya." *Paléorient* 7 (1): 107–22.

———. 1982. "The Role of the Indo-Iranian Borderlands in the Formation of the Harappan Writing System." *Annali dell'Istituto Orientali di Napoli* 42:513–19.

———. 2014. *Nomadism in Iran: From Antiquity to the Modern Era.* New York: Oxford University Press.

———. 2016. *The Archaeology of Elam: Formation and Transformation of an Ancient Iranian State.* 2nd rev. ed. Cambridge: Cambridge University Press.

———. 2018a. "The Epithet 'Sister's Son' in Ancient Elam: Aspects of the Avunculate in Cross-Cultural Perspective." In *Grenzüberschreitungen. Festschrift für Hans Neumann zum 65. Geburtstag am 9. Mai 2018*, edited by K. Kleber, G. Neumann, and S. Paulus, 523–55. Münster: Dubsar 5.

———. 2018b. "Bīsotūn and the French Enlightenment." *JRAS* 28:583–614.

———. 2022a. *Persia Portrayed: Envoys to the West, 1600–1842.* Washington, DC: Mage.

———. 2022b. *Agreeable News from Persia: Iran in the Colonial and Early Republican American Press, 1712–1848.* 3 vols. Wiesbaden: Universal- und kulturhistorische Studien.

———. 2022c. "Antoine-Isaac Silvestre De Sacy and the Study of Tāq-E Bostān." *Sasanian Studies/Sasanidische Studien* 1:243–57.

Pourshariati, P. 2008. *Decline and Fall of the Sasanian Empire: The Sasanian-Parthian Confederacy and the Arab Conquest of Iran.* London: I.B. Tauris.

———. 2017. "Kārin." *Encyclopædia Iranica*, online edition, www.iranicaonline.org/articles/karin.

Prášek, J. D. 1913. "Kambyses." *Der Alte Orient* 14 (2): 3–31.

Prestwich, M. 2003. "Feudalism." In *The Social Science Encyclopedia*, 2nd ed., edited by A. Kuper and J. Kuper, 300–302. London: Routledge.

Puukko, A. F. 1949. "Die Leviratsehe in den altorientalischen Gesetzen." *ArOr* 17:296–99.

Quatremère, E.-M. 1811. *Mémoires géographiques et historiques sur l'Égypte, et sur quelques contrées voisines.* Vol. 2. Paris: F. Schœll.

———. 1840. Review of J. Mohl, *Le Livre des Rois, par Abou' lkasim Firdousi. Journal des savants 1840*: 337–53.

Quinault, P. 1659. *Le mariage de Cambise, tragi-comedie.* Paris: Guillaume de Luyne.

Quintana, E. 2010. "Filiacion y acceso al trono en Elam (2ª mitad II milenio A.C.)." *RA* 104:45–63.

———. 2016. "The Elamite Family (Royal Family, Adoptions)." *Mundo Elamita*, no. 2: www.um.es/cepoat/elamita/wp-content/uploads/2018/03/The-Elamite-Family.pdf.

Radcliffe-Brown, A. R. 1950. Introduction to *African Systems of Kinship and Marriage*, edited by A. R. Radcliffe-Brown and D. Forde, 1–85. London: Oxford University Press and International African Institute.

Radcliffe-Brown, A. R., and D. Forde, eds. 1950. *African Systems of Kinship and Marriage.* London: Oxford University Press and International African Institute.

Radner, K. 2003. "An Assyrian View on the Medes." In *Continuity of empire (?): Assyria, Media, Persia,* edited by G. B. Lanfranchi, M. Roaf, and R. Rollinger, 37–64. Padua: History of the Ancient Near East/Monograph 5.

———. 2013. "Assyria and the Medes." In *The Oxford Handbook of Ancient Iran,* edited by D. T. Potts, 442–56. New York: Oxford University Press.

Rapp, A. 1866. "Die Religion und Sitte der Perser und übrigen Iranier nach den griechischen und römischen Quellen." *ZDMG* 20:49–140.

Renan, E. 1882. *Qu'est-ce qu'une nation? Conférence faite en Sorbonne, le 11 Mars 1882.* 2nd ed. Paris: Calmann Lévy.

Reynolds, S. 2017. "The History of the Idea of Lehnswesen." *German Historical Institute London Bulletin* 39 (2): 3–20.

Roaf, M. 2017. "Kassite and Elamite Kings." In *Karduniaš. Babylonia under the Kassites,* edited by A. Bartelmus and K. Sternitzke, 166–95. New York: de Gruyter.

Ross, E. D. 1930. "The Orkhon Inscriptions: Being a Translation of Vilhelm Thomsen's Final Danish Rendering." *BSOS* 5 (4): 861–76.

Roth, M. T. 1989/1990. "The Material Composition of the Neo-Babylonian Dowry." *Archiv für Orientforschung* 36/37:1–55.

———. 1995. *Law Collections from Mesopotamia and Asia Minor.* Atlanta: Writings from the Ancient World 6.

Rowley, H. H. 1947. "The Marriage of Ruth." *Harvard Theological Review* 40 (2): 77–99.

Sadafi, S. J. 2013. "Prosopographische Untersuchungen anhand der Rechtsurkunden aus Susa." In De Graef and Tavernier 2013, 355–64.

Sahlins, M. 1965. "On the Ideology and Composition of Descent Groups." *Man* 65:104–7.

———. 1976. *Culture and Practical Reason.* Chicago: University of Chicago Press.

Saint-Martin, A.-J. 1850. *Fragments d'une histoire des Arsacides, ouvrage posthume.* Vol. 1. Paris: Imprimerie Nationale.

Sallaberger, W. 1996. *Der babylonische Töpfer und seine Gefäße: Nach Urkunden altsumerischer bis altbabylonischer Zeit sowie lexikalischen und literarischen Zeugnissen.* Gent: Mesopotamian History and Environment 2/3.

Sancisi-Weerdenburg, H. 1983. "Exit Atossa: Images of women in Greek Historiography on Persia." In *Images of Women in Antiquity,* edited by A. Cameron and A. Kuhrt, 20–33. Detroit: Wayne State University Press.

Sanjana, D. D. P. 1888. "On the Alleged Practice of Next-of-Kin Marriages in Old Irân." *Journal of the Bombay Branch of the Royal Asiatic Society* 17:97–136.

Sapir, E. 1916. "Terms of Relationship and the Levirate." *AA* 18:327–37.

Sarre, F., and E. Herzfeld. 1910. *Iranische Felsreliefs.* Berlin: Ernst Wasmuth.

Scarisbrick, D. 1986. "The Devonshire Parure." *Archaeologia* 108:239–54.

Schaeder, H. H. 1936. "Ein parthischer Titel im Sogdischen." *BSOAS* 8:737–49.

Scheftelowitz, I. 1915. "Die Leviratsehe." *Archiv für Religionswissenschaft* 18:250–56.

Scheil, V. 1900. *Textes élamites-sémitiques, première série.* Paris: MDP 2.

———. 1901. *Textes élamites-anzanites, première série.* Paris: MDP 3.

———. 1905. "Miscellen V. Ḫapirti ou Ḫatamti?" *OLZ* 8:203.

———. 1907. *Textes élamites-anzanites, troisième série.* Paris: MDP 9.

———. 1911. *Textes élamites-anzanites, quatrième série.* Paris: MDP 11.

——. 1939. "Fraternité et solidarité à Suse au temps de Sirukduḫ." In *Symbolae ad iura orientis antiqui pertinentes Paulo Koschaker dedicatae*, edited by T. Folkers, J. Friedrich, J. G. Lautner, and J. C. Miles, 106–7. Leiden: Brill.

Schindel, N. 2004. *Sylloge Nummorum Sasanidarum Paris—Berlin—Wien. Band III/1. Shapur II.—Kawad I./2. Regierung*. Vienna: Denkschriften der Österreichischen Akademie der Wissenschaften, phil.-hist. Kl. 325.

Schlichtegroll, F. 1798. *Choix des principales pierres gravées de la collection qui appartenait autrefois au Baron de Stosch et qui se trouve maintenant dans le Cabinet du Roi de Prusse*. Nürnberg: Jean Frédéric Frauenholz.

Schmidt, E. F. 1970. *Persepolis III: The Royal Tombs and Other Monuments*. Chicago: Oriental Institute of the University of Chicago.

Schmitt, R. 1983. "Sūrēn, aber Kārin. Zu den Namen zweier Parthergeschlechter." *Münchener Studien zur Sprachwissenschaft* 42:197–205.

——. 1991. *The Bisitun Inscriptions of Darius the Great, Old Persian Text*. London: Corpus Inscriptionum Iranicarum 1.

——. 2002. "Onomastische Bemerkungen zu der Namenliste des Fravardīn Yašt." In *Religious Themes and Texts of Pre-Islamic Iran and Central Asia: Studies in Honour of Professor Gherardo Gnoli on the Occasion of His 65th Birthday on 6th December 2002*, edited by C. G. Cereti, M. Maggi, and E. Provasi, 363–74. Wiesbaden: Dr. Ludwig Reichert.

——. 2009. *Die altpersischen Inschriften der Achaimeniden: Editio minor mit deutscher Übersetzung*. Wiesbaden: Reichert.

——. 2011a. *Iranische Personennamen in der griechischen Literatur vor Alexander d. Gr.* Vienna: Iranisches Personennamenbuch 5/5A [= Sitzungsberichte der Österreichischen Akademie der Wissenschaften, phil.-hist. Kl. 823].

——. 2011b. "Darius VI: Achaemenid Princes." *Encyclopædia Iranica*, online edition, www.iranicaonline.org/articles/darius-vi.

Schneider, D. M. 1967. "Kinship and Culture: Descent and Filiation as Cultural Constructs." *Southwestern Journal of Anthropology* 23:65–73.

Scott, L. 2005. *Historical Commentary on Herodotus Book 6*. Leiden: Mnemosyne Supplement 26.

Seligman, B. Z. 1929. "Incest and Descent: Their Influence on Social Organization." *JRAI* 59:231–72.

——. 1935. "The Incest Taboo as a Social Regulation." *Sociological Review* 27:75–93.

Sellwood, D., P. Whitting, and R. Williams. 1985. *An Introduction to Sasanian Coins*. London: Spink & Son.

Service, E. R. 1960. "Kinship Terminology and Evolution." *AA* 62:747–63.

Shahbazi, S. 2016. "Bahrām I." *Encyclopædia Iranica*, online edition, www.iranicaonline.org/articles/bahram-01.

Shahshahani, S. 2003. "The Mamassani of Iran: At the Juncture of Two Modes of Subsistence." *Nomadic Peoples*, n.s., 7:87–97.

Shaw, I., and R. Jameson. 1993. "Amethyst Mining in the Eastern Desert: A Preliminary Survey at Wadi el-Hudi." *Journal of Egyptian Archaeology* 79:81–97.

Shayegan, M. R. 2010. "Nugae Epigraphicae." *BAI* 19:169–79.

Shenkar, M. 2017. "The Headdress of the Tilly Tepe 'Prince.'" *Ancient Civilizations from Scythia to Siberia* 23:151–83.

Shokoohy, M. 1994. "Sasanian Royal Emblems and Their Reemergence in the Fourteenth-Century Deccan." *Muqarnas* 11:65–78.

Silvestre de Sacy, A. I. 1793. *Mémoires sur diverse antiquités de la Perse, et sur les médailles des rois de la dynastie des Sassanides; suivis de l'histoire de cette dynastie, traduite du Persan de Mirkhond.* Paris: Imprimerie Nationale exécutive du Louvre.

———. 1801. "Observations sur quelques médailles et pierres gravées qui portent des légendes en caractères pehlvi ou ancien persan; par sir W. Ouseley." *Magasin encyclopédique ou Journal des sciences, lettres et des arts* 3:354–63.

———. 1815. "Mémoire sur les monumens et les inscriptions de Kirmanschah et de Bi-Sutoun, et sur divers autres monumens Sassanides." *Histoire et mémoires de l'Institut Royal de France, classe d'histoire et de littérature ancienne* 12:162–242.

Sinisi, F. 2012. *Sylloge Nummorum Parthicorum.* Vol. 7, *Vologases I–Pacorus II.* Vienna: Österreichische Akademie der Wissenschaften.

Skjærvø, P. O. 2007. "A Postscript on 'The Seal of a Eunuch in the Sasanian Court.'" *Journal of Inner Asian Art and Archaeology* 2:39.

———. 2011/2012. "Kartir." *Encyclopædia Iranica,* online edition, www.iranicaonline.org/articles/kartir.

———. 2012. "Jamšid i. Myth of Jamšid." *Encyclopædia Iranica,* online edition, www.iranicaonline.org/articles/jamsid-i.

———. 2013. "Marriage ii. Next of Kin Marriage in Zoroastrianism." *Encyclopædia Iranica,* online edition, www.iranicaonline.org/articles/marriage-next-of-kin.

Soane, E. B. 1914. *To Mesopotamia and Kurdistan in Disguise, with Historical Notices of the Kurdish Tribes and the Chaldeans of Kurdistan.* Boston: Small, Maynard.

Soldt, W. H. van. 1990. "Matrilinearität. A. In Elam." *RlA* 7:586–88.

Soudavar, A. 2009. "The Vocabulary and Syntax of Iconography in Sasanian Iran." *IrAnt* 44:417–60.

———. 2014. *Mithraic Societies: From Brotherhood Ideal to Religion's Adversary.* Houston, TX: A. Soudavar.

Spek, R. J. van der. 1985. Review of G. F. Seibt, *Griechische Söldner im Achaimenidenreich. Mnemosyne* 38:254–56.

Spier, J. 2011. "Late Antique and Early Christian Gems: Some Unpublished Examples." In Entwistle and Adams 2011, 193–207.

Stayt, H. A. 1931. *The Bavenda.* Oxford: Oxford University Press.

Steinkeller, P. 2013. "Puzur-Inšušinak at Susa: A Pivotal Episode of Early Elamite History Reconsidered." In De Graef and Tavernier 2013, 293–317.

Stern, B. J. 1930. "Selections from the Letters of Lorimer Fison and A. W. Howitt to Lewis Henry Morgan." *AA* 32:257–79.

Stol, M. 2016. *Women in the Ancient Near East.* Berlin: de Gruyter.

Stolper, M. W. 1985. *Entrepreneurs and Empire: The Murašû Archive, the Murašû Firm, and Persian Rule in Babylonia.* Leiden: PIHANS 54.

———. 1987–90. "Malamīr. B. Philologisch." *RlA* 7:276–81.

Stone, L. 1972. "Prosopography." *Daedalus* 100:46–79.

Stoneman, R. 2015. *Xerxes, a Persian Life.* New Haven, CT: Yale University Press.

Sumner, W. M. 1977. "Early Settlements in Fars Province, Iran." In *Mountains and Lowlands: Essays in the Archaeology of Greater Mesopotamia,* edited by L. D. Levine and T. C. Young Jr., 291–305. Malibu: Undena.

Sumner, W. M. 1988. "Prelude to Proto-Elamite Anshan: The Lapui Phase." *IrAnt* 23:23–43.

Sykes, M. 1908. "The Kurdish Tribes of the Ottoman Empire." *JRAI* 38:451–86.

Syvänne, I., and K. Maksymiuk. 2018. *The Military History of the Third Century Iran.* Siedlce: Scientific Publishing House of Siedlce University of Natural Sciences and Humanities.

Szemerényi, O. 1977. "Studies in the Kinship Terminology of the Indo-European Languages with Special Reference to Indian, Iranian, Greek, and Latin." In *Varia 1977*, edited by J. Duchesne-Guillemin and J. Kellens, 1–240. Tehran-Liège: Acta Iranica 3rd Ser. 16 [= Textes et Mémoires 7].

Talbot, J. 1861. "Proceedings at Meetings of the Archaeological Institute. May 3rd, 1861." *Archaeological Journal* 18:268–306.

Tancoigne, M. 1820. *A Narrative of a Journey into Persia, and Residence at Teheran . . .* London: William Wright.

Tassie, J., and R. E. Raspe. 1791. *A Descriptive Catalogue of a General Collection of Ancient and Modern Engraved Gems, Cameos as Well as Intaglios . . .* 2 vols. London: Tassie and Murray.

Thomas, E. 1866. "Sassanian Gems and Early Armenian Coins." *Numismatic Chronicle and Journal of the Numismatic Society*, n.s., 6:241–48.

———. 1868a. "Sassanian Inscriptions." *JRAS* 3:241–358.

———. 1868b. *Early Sassanian Inscriptions, Seals and Coins.* London: Trübner.

———. 1873a. *Numismatic and Other Antiquarian Illustrations of the Rule of the Sassanians in Persia, A.D. 226 to 652.* London: Trübner.

———. 1873b. "Sassanian Coins (Continued)." *Numismatic Chronicle and Journal of the Numismatic Society* 13:220–53.

Thomas, L. 2018. "Königs- und Nachfolgermord im Achaimenidenreich." *Marburger Beiträge zur antiken Handels-, Wirtschafts- und Sozialgeschichte* 35:1–86.

Tilly, C. 1984. "The Old New Social History and the New Old Social History." *Review* 7: 363–406.

Tritton, A. S., and H. A. R. Gibb. 1933. "The First and Second Crusades from an Anonymous Syriac Chronicle." *JRAS* 65 (2): 69–101, 273–305.

Tuplin, C. 2010. "All the King's Men." In *The World of Achaemenid Persia: History, Art and Society in Iran and the Ancient Near East*, edited by J. Curtis and St. J. Simpson, 51–61. London: I.B. Tauris.

Tylor, E. B. 1889. "On a Method of Investigating the Development of Institutions: Applied to Laws of Marriage and Descent." *JRAI* 18:245–72.

Urban, G. 1996. *Metaphysical Community: The Interplay of the Senses and the Intellect.* Austin: University of Texas Press.

Vallat, F. 1980. *Suse et l'Elam.* Paris: Recherches sur les grandes civilisations.

———. 1985. "Hutelutuš-Inšušinak et la famille royale élamite." *RA* 79:43–50.

———. 1996. "L'Élam à l'époque paléo-Babylonienne et ses relations avec la Mésopotamie." In *Mari, Ébla et les Hourrites, dix ans de travaux, première partie*, edited by J.-M. Durand, 297–319. Paris: Amurru 1.

———. 1997. "Cyrus l'usurpateur." *Topoi Supplement* 1:423–34.

———. 2002. "Les prétendus fonctionnaires Unsak des textes néo-élamites et achéménides." *ARTA* 2002.006. www.achemenet.com/pdf/arta/2002.006.pdf.

Vanden Berghe, L. 1983. *Reliefs rupestres de l'Irān ancien.* Brussels: Musées royaux d'Art et d'Histoire.

Vandiver, P. 1987. "Sequential Slab Construction: A Conservative Southwest Asiatic Ceramic Tradition, ca. 7000–3000 B.C." *Paléorient* 13:9–35.

Vannicelli, P. 2012. "The Mythical Origins of the Medes and the Persians." In *Myth, Truth, and Narrative in Herodotus*, edited by E. Baragwanath and M. de Bakker, 255–68. Oxford: Oxford University Press.

Vanstiphout, H. L. J. 1983. "Problems in the 'Matter of Aratta.'" *Iraq* 45:35–42.

Vernier, B. 2005. "La prohibition des rapports sexuels et matrimoniaux avec les proches parents et alliés. Pour une théorie unitaire (1)." *Regards sociologiques* 30:30–60.

Vevaina, Y. S-D. 2018. "A Father, a Daughter, and a Son-in-Law in Zoroastrian Hermeneutics." In *Sasanian Iran in the Context of Late Antiquity: The Bahari Lecture Series at the University of Oxford*, edited by T. Daryaee, 121–47. Irvine, CA: Ancient Iran Series 6.

Voigt, M. M., and R. H. Dyson Jr. 1992. "The Chronology of Iran, ca. 8000–2000 B.C." In *Chronologies in Old World Archaeology*. 3rd ed. Vol. 1, edited by R. W. Ehrich, 122–53. Chicago: University of Chicago Press.

Volgger, D. 2002. "Dtn 25,5-10—Per Gesetz zur Ehe gezwungen?" *Biblische Notizen* 114/115:173–88.

Waetzoldt, H. 1970–71. "Zwei unveröffentlichte Ur-III-Texte über die Herstellung von Tongefäßen." *Welt des Orients* 6:7–41.

Waterfield, R., trans. 2019. *Diodorus of Sicily. The Library, Books 16–20: Philip II, Alexander the Great, and the Successors*. Oxford: Oxford World's Classics.

Waters, M. W. 2000. *A Survey of Neo-Elamite History*. Helsinki: State Archives of Assyria Studies.

———. 2004. "Cyrus and the Achaemenids." *Iran* 42:91–102.

Watson, J. S. 1853. *Epitome of the Philippic History of Pompeius Trogus*. London: Henry G. Bohn.

Weeks, L. R., K. Alizadeh, L. Niakan, K. Alamdari, M. Zeidi, A. Khosrowzadeh, and B. McCall. 2006. "The Neolithic Settlement of Highland SW Iran: New Evidence from the Mamasani District." *Iran* 44:1–31.

Weeks, L. R., C. A. Petrie, and D. T. Potts. 2010. "Ubaid-Related-Related? The 'Black-on-Buff' Ceramic Tradition of Highland Southwest Iran." In *Beyond the Ubaid: Transformation and Integration in the Prehistoric Societies of the Middle East*, edited by R. A. Carter and G. Philip, 247–78. Chicago: SAOC 63.

Weisberg, D. E. 2009. *Levirate Marriage and the Family in Ancient Judaism*. Lebanon, NH: Brandeis University Press / University Press of New England.

Welles, C. B. 1963. *Diodorus of Sicily*. Vol. 8. Cambridge, MA: Harvard University Press / London: William Heinemann.

West, E. W. 1882. *Pahlavi Texts. Part II: The Dâdistân-î Dînîk and the Epistles of Mânûskîhar*. Oxford: Clarendon Press.

Westbrook, R. 1991. *Property and the Family in Biblical Law*. Sheffield, UK: Sheffield Academic Press.

Westropp, H. M. 1874. *A Manual of Precious Stones and Antique Gems*. London: Sampson Low, Marston, Low, & Searle.

White, L. A. 1958. "What Is a Classificatory Kinship Term?" *Journal of Anthropological Research* 14:378–85.

White, S. 2005. *Re-thinking Kinship and Feudalism in Early Medieval Europe*. Aldershot: Ashgate Variorum.

Wicks, Y. 2019. *Profiling Death: Neo-Elamite Mortuary Practices, Afterlife Beliefs, and Entanglements with Ancestors*. Leiden: Brill.

Widengren, G. 1956. "Recherches sur le féodalisme iranien." *Orientalia Suecana* 5:79–182.

———. 1969. *Der Feudalismus im alten Iran. Männerbund—Gefolgswesen—Feudalismus in der iranischen Gesellschaft im Hinblick auf die indogermanischen Verhältnisse*. Cologne: Wissenschaftliche Abhandlungen der Arbeitsgemeinschaft für Forschung des Landes Nordrhein-Westfalen 40.

Wiesehöfer, J. 2001. *Ancient Persia from 550 BC to 650 AD*. London: I.B. Tauris.

———. 2010. "King and Kingship in the Sasanian Empire." In *Concepts of Kingship in Antiquity*, edited by G. B. Lanfranchi and R. Rollinger, 135–52. Padua: HANE/M 11.

Wilson, A. T. 1908. "Notes on a Journey from Bandar Abbas to Shiraz viâ Lar, in February and March, 1907." *GJ* 31:152–69.

Wilson, J. D., and C. Roehrborn. 1999. "Long-Term Consequences of Castration in Men: Lessons from the Skoptzy and the Eunuchs of the Chinese and Ottoman Courts." *Journal of Clinical Endocrinology & Metabolism* 84:4324–31.

Winckelmann, J. J. 1760. *Description des pierres gravées du seu Baron de Stosch*. Florence: André Bonducci.

Winckler, H. 1901a. Review of Scheil, MDP 2. *OLZ* 4:412–15, 448–53.

———. 1901b. "Das alte Westasien." In *Weltgeschichte. Dritter Band, Westasien und Afrika*, edited by H. Winckler, H. Schurtz, and C. Niebuhr, 3–248. Leipzig: Bibliographisches Institut.

Wolff, E. 1964. "Das Weib des Masistes." *Hermes* 92:51–58.

Wolski, J. 1967. "L'aristocratie parthe et les commencements du féodalisme en Iran." *IrAnt* 7:133–44.

———. 1989. "Die gesellschaftliche und politische Stellung der großen parthischen Familien." *Tyche: Beiträge zur Alten Geschichte, Papyrologie und Epigraphik* 4:221–27.

Wunsch, C. 2005. "The Šangû-Ninurta Archive." In *Approaching the Babylonian economy*, edited by H. D. Baker and M. Jursa, 365–416. Münster: AOAT 330 [= Veröffentlichungen zur Wirtschaftsgeschichte Babyloniens im 1. Jahrtausend v. Chr. 2].

———. 2007. "The Egibi Family." In *The Babylonian World*, edited by G. Leick, 232–43. New York: Routledge.

Yardley, J. C., and W. Heckel 1997. *Justin, Epitome of the Philippic History of Pompeius Trogus Books 11–12: Alexander the Great*. Oxford: Clarendon Press.

Yatsenko, S. A. 2010a. "Problems and Study Methods of the Ancient and Early Medieval Iranian-Speaking Peoples' Nishan-Signs." In *Traditional Marking Systems: A Preliminary Survey*, edited by J. E. Pim, S. A. Yatsenko, and O. Perrin, 111–31. London: Dunkling Books.

———. 2010b. "Marks of the Ancient and Early Medieval Iranian-Speaking Peoples of Iran, Eastern Europe, Transoxiana and South Siberia." In *Traditional Marking Systems: A Preliminary Survey*, edited by J. E. Pim, S. A. Yatsenko, and O. Perrin, 133–54. London: Dunkling Books.

Yusifov, Y. B. 1974. "The Problem of the Order of Succession in Elam Again." *AAASH* 22:321–31.

Zadok, R. 2011. "The Babylonia-Elam Connections in the Chaldaean and Achaemenid Periods (Part One)." *Tel Aviv* 38:120–43.

Zakharov, A. A. 1933. "Materials for the Corpus Sigillorum Asiæ Minoris Antiquæ II." *Archív Orientální* 5:270–72.

Zehbari, Z., R. Mehr Afarin, and S. R. Musavi Haji. 2015. "Studies on the Structural Characteristics of Achaemenid Pottery from Dahan-E Gholaman." *Ancient Near Eastern Studies* 52:217–59.

Zimmer, H. 1894. "Das Mutterrecht der Pikten und seine Bedeutung für die arische Alterthumswissenschaft." *Zeitschrift der Savigny-Stiftung für Rechtsgeschichte: Romanistische Abteilung* 4:209–40.

Zschokke, H. 1883. *Das Weib im Alten Testamente.* Vienna: Heinrich Kirsch.

Zwierlein-Diehl, E. 2011. "Gem Portraits of Soldier-Emperors." In Entwistle and Adams 2011, 149–62.

INDEX

Founded in 1893,
UNIVERSITY OF CALIFORNIA PRESS
publishes bold, progressive books and journals
on topics in the arts, humanities, social sciences,
and natural sciences—with a focus on social
justice issues—that inspire thought and action
among readers worldwide.

The UC PRESS FOUNDATION
raises funds to uphold the press's vital role
as an independent, nonprofit publisher, and
receives philanthropic support from a wide
range of individuals and institutions—and from
committed readers like you. To learn more, visit
ucpress.edu/supportus.